THE NEGRO LEAGUES

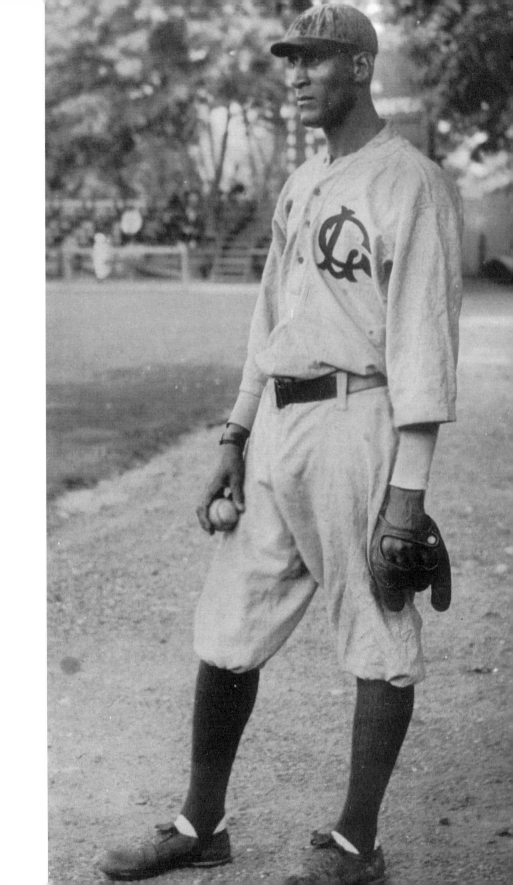

AFRICAN-AMERICAN ACHIEVERS

THE NEGRO LEAGUES

James A. Riley

CHELSEA HOUSE PUBLISHERS
Philadelphia

To Josh, without whose help this book would not have been possible.

Chelsea House Publishers
Editorial Director Richard Rennert
Production Manager Pamela Loos
Art Director Sara Davis
Picture Editor Judy Hasday

Staff for THE NEGRO LEAGUES
Senior Editor John Ziff
Associate Editor Therese DeAngelis
Editorial Assistant Kristine Brennan
Designer Takeshi Takahashi
Picture Researcher Alan Gottlieb
Cover Design Alison Burnside
Digital Photo Colorization Robert Gerson

First Printing

1 3 5 7 9 8 6 4 2

Library of Congress Cataloging-in-Publication Data

Riley, James A.
The Negro leagues / James A. Riley.
   p. cm. — (African-American achievers)
Summary: Provides a history of the Negro leagues and the
role they played in integrating baseball.

ISBN 0-7910-2591-8. — ISBN 0-7910-2592-6 (pbk.)

1. Negro leagues—History—Juvenile literature. [1. Negro
leagues—History. 2. Baseball—History.] I. Title. II. Series.
GV875.N35R45 1996
796.357'64'0973—dc20   95-46411
                                                       CIP
                                                        AC

Frontispiece: *Smokey Joe
Williams (also known as Cyclone
Joe Williams), one of the greatest
black pitchers of all time.*

On the cover: *The 1944 Homestead Grays.*

CONTENTS

AFRICAN-AMERICAN ACHIEVERS

Prologue

On APRIL 15, 1947, baseball—and America—changed forever. At Ebbets Field in Brooklyn a crowd of 26,623 watched as Jackie Robinson took the field for the Dodgers, marking the first time since 1884 that an African American appeared in a major league game. Baseball's "color line," created by a so-called gentlemen's agreement between club owners not to hire black players, was at last broken.

But while Robinson's entrance into the major leagues marked the beginning of one era in baseball, it also spelled the beginning of the end of another. As black stars followed in his footsteps and major league baseball gradually became desegregated, the Negro leagues, which had for so long been the only avenue open to black players, faded away.

Since 1920 African Americans had played baseball—and played it with distinction—in professional leagues of their own. No less talented than their white counterparts, they had lost out on the chance to prove their skill alongside major leaguers because of the nation's racist attitudes. But the black ballplayers were not the only ones who lost out. As Monte Irvin, who began his career in the Negro leagues and went on to stardom in the majors, put it, "The real losers in the years prior to Jackie Robinson's breaking of the color line are the many millions of fans who were deprived of the opportunity of seeing the great black players from the first half of the twentieth century."

1

In the Beginning (1868–1899)

IN THE AFTERMATH of the Civil War, baseball enjoyed a great surge in popularity as a country weary of four years of bloodshed embraced peacetime diversions. Americans of all races and creeds joined in the game that became our national pastime. Some black Americans played on all-black ballclubs, others on integrated teams. Baseball was still an amateur sport, and the National Association of Baseball Players represented most of the top ballclubs. But just as prejudice remained in the society at large, it contaminated the game's governing body. On December 11, 1868, the association held its annual convention in Philadelphia and unanimously voted to bar "any club which may be composed of one or more colored persons." This was the first appearance of an official "color line" in baseball.

The next spring, the Cincinnati Red Stockings fielded the first professional baseball team, and most of the leading ballclubs soon followed Cincinnati into the pro ranks. Because professional teams and leagues were not bound by the amateur association's official position regarding black players, black Americans continued to play alongside their white counterparts on integrated professional ballclubs. And in some instances entire black teams played in

Moses Fleetwood Walker, the first African American to play major league baseball, starred for the Toledo ballclub of the American Association in 1884.

otherwise all-white leagues. Although these practices were not commonplace, they continued
throughout the first quarter-century of professional
baseball.

During this time John W. Jackson, who played
baseball under the name Bud Fowler, became the
first black professional baseball player. Ironically,
Fowler spent much of his childhood in Coopers-
town, New York, where tradition insists the game of
baseball was first played. By some accounts Fowler
began his career as early as 1872, but his first docu-
mented appearance was in 1878 with the Chelsea,
Massachusetts, ballclub. Fowler continued playing
on integrated teams through 1895 and was often
joined by other top black players of the era.

Of the black players of the 19th century, Frank
Grant is considered the best. Grant played amateur
ball before turning pro in 1886. Like Jackie Robinson, he was a second baseman and as such was frequently spiked by white base runners who objected
to the presence of black ballplayers. To protect
himself against these "high spikes," Grant resorted
to wearing shin guards in the field.

Two years before Grant began his professional
career, another black baseball pioneer, Moses Fleetwood Walker, became the first black major league
baseball player, preceding Jackie Robinson by 63
years. Walker was born in 1857 in Mount Pleasant,
Ohio, a small village that had served as a way station
on the Underground Railroad for fugitive slaves.
After spending his formative years in Steubenville,
Ohio, he entered college and eventually attended
law school at the University of Michigan.

Early in his baseball career, Walker played with a
semipro club in Cleveland. When the team played
a game in Louisville, Kentucky, he got his first real
taste of the type of prejudice that he would
encounter in his travels: the Louisville manager
insisted that Walker not be allowed to play because

of his race. Although Cleveland's manager vigor-ously protested the disqualification of his star catch-er, the umpire ruled in favor of the home team.

Walker's replacement suffered such badly bruised hands that he refused to continue after the first inning. The game was halted, and the 3,000 restless fans yelled at the umpire to let Walker play. Sensing the mood of the crowd and concerned with the possibility of losing the proceeds from the gate, the Louisville club's vice president tried to persuade Walker to take the field. Walker, still simmering from the slight he had already suffered, reluctantly consented. The fans cheered and called his name as he walked past the grandstands.

However, the crowd's feelings were not shared

John W. Jackson, who played amateur and professional baseball under the name Bud Fowler (standing, center), with white teammates. In the early days of baseball, integrated teams were not uncommon.

by the Louisville ballclub, whose two best players walked off the field in protest. Louisville's manager renewed his demand that Walker be barred, and the umpire again removed the star catcher from the field. Though the decision placated the Louisville team, the hometown fans were outraged. For the remainder of the game, the crowd booed and jeered the Louisville players and openly cheered for the visitors. Despite the fan support, without Walker behind the plate Cleveland lost by a score of 6-3.

In spite of this unpleasant experience, Walker continued his baseball pursuits and entered the professional ranks. Three years later, in 1884, he made his major league debut with the Toledo ballclub of the American Association. In professional baseball, he again encountered resistance to his presence in the lineup. In his home park, he was generally well received by players and spectators, but on the road he was subjected to harassment, verbal abuse, and anonymous threats of violence.

While most of Walker's teammates were supportive, Toledo's ace pitcher, Tony Mullane, was an exception. His dislike of blacks led him to refuse to take signs from Walker. In fact, Mullane often deliberately tried to cross up his catcher by throwing pitches different from those Walker had signaled. Eventually Walker had had enough, and during one game he walked out to the mound and told the star hurler, "Mr. Mullane, I'll catch you without signals, but I won't catch you if you are going to cross me when I give you a signal." Then he turned and walked back behind the plate, and for the rest of the season he caught Mullane without knowing what pitch was coming.

Although he was a skilled catcher, Walker was hard-pressed to survive under this arrangement. Later in the year he suffered a cracked rib from a foul tip and was released from the team in early September. He continued playing in the minor leagues

for several years, but he never again returned to the major leagues.

Walker's pioneering entrance failed to open the major leagues to the host of other talented African-American players. In fact, only his brother Welday, who joined Fleetwood on the Toledo ballclub later in 1884 and left after that season, was to follow him. In contrast to Jackie Robinson, Fleetwood Walker, the first black major leaguer, is today virtually forgotten, a footnote in baseball history.

The long-range effect of Walker's exit from the major leagues was not immediately apparent. Blacks continued playing on integrated teams in organized baseball, with 1887 being the high-water mark. That year more African Americans played on minor

The Oberlin club. Seated at the left is Moses Fleetwood Walker. His brother Welday (standing, second from right) also had a brief major league career.

league clubs than at any other time until after Jackie Robinson broke the color barrier 60 years later.

However, the 1887 season also saw an increase in racial tension, as more teams refused to play games involving black players. Cap Anson, the era's superstar and manager of the Chicago White Stockings, the defending champions of the National League, was foremost in this regard. He refused to let his team play an exhibition game against the Newark ballclub if they used their ace pitcher, George Stovey. Newark's manager gave in to the threat, and Stovey was withheld from the game because of "illness." Four years earlier, Anson had unsuccessfully tried the same tactic to prevent Fleetwood Walker from playing an exhibition game against his White Stockings.

These demands set the stage for future exclusion of blacks from the established leagues. On July 14, 1887, the International League, one of the most integrated leagues in existence at the time, officially drew a color line by voting not to approve any new contracts with black players. This left black players more dependent on all-black teams for employment.

The first black professional team was formed in the summer of 1885, only a year after Fleetwood Walker's departure from the major leagues. The club had its origins in a team organized to play for the entertainment of summer guests at a Long Island hotel. Called the Argyle Hotel Athletics, the team essentially consisted of the Philadelphia Keystones, an outstanding amateur club whose members doubled as waiters at the hotel.

Encouraged by their success at the hotel, the team members decided to try their luck as a traveling professional ballclub. Under the management of white entrepreneur John F. Lang, the club added star players from other teams to its roster and began touring. Recognizing the antiblack racial bias of the

The Page Fence Giants, an all-black professional team, were organized as a promotional stunt. They traveled by railroad throughout the United States and Canada, entertaining fans with a combination of skillful baseball and comedic antics. The 1895 club, pictured here, compiled an impressive record of 118 wins, 36 losses, and 2 ties.

times, the players concluded that it would be advantageous to pass themselves off as Cubans. So the team was renamed the Cuban Giants, and the players spoke a gibberish on the field that they hoped would be mistaken for Spanish.

Under Lang's ownership, the Cuban Giants emerged as the strongest independent team in the East. One of the teams that they played during their initial barnstorming tour was the major league New York Metropolitans, seventh-place finishers in the American Association that season. Although the Giants lost the encounter by a score of 11-3, they demonstrated that they could play on the same field with major leaguers.

After one season, Lang sold the team to another white businessman, Walter Cook, who in turn hired a black manager, S. K. Govern. By traveling, the team gained more exposure and progressively attracted higher-quality ballplayers. Within a short time the Cuban Giants were nearing parity with the best major league white teams.

The players received their expenses and a weekly salary based on their playing position. Pitchers

The Cuban X-Giants dominated black professional baseball from the mid-1890s to the early 1900s. Despite the team's name, the players were African Americans—the idea of passing for Cubans had occurred to the team's predecessor, the Cuban Giants, whose players believed color-conscious America would more readily accept them.

and catchers were paid $18; infielders, $15; and outfielders, $12. But top black players were still able to make more money playing on predominantly white teams in white leagues, and like other black clubs, the Cuban Giants lost many stars to white teams. Nevertheless, the Giants managed to field a superior ballclub, and in 1887 they defeated two white major league clubs, the Cincinnati and Indianapolis teams of the National League. Showing further proof that they were on a par with the best white teams, the Cuban Giants lost a hard-fought 6-4 game to the Detroit ballclub, the National League champions.

Across the country, interest and participation in baseball was on the rise among African Americans. New amateur and professional leagues sprang up but never really took root. The Cuban Giants, the top black team of the era, did not join these fledgling leagues because their owners knew they could make more money playing as an independent team.

The Giants' domination of black baseball continued into 1888, when the four top professional teams held a challenge tournament to determine the Colored Championship of America. Cuban Giants co-owner J. M. Bright donated the championship trophy, a silver ball, which his team proceeded to win.

During the next three years, the Cuban Giants played in integrated leagues. In 1889 the Giants and the New York Gorhams, another of the earliest professional black teams, joined six white clubs in forming the Middle States League. The Cuban Giants represented Trenton, New Jersey; the Gorhams, Philadelphia. The next year the Cuban Giants moved to York, Pennsylvania, and played as the York Monarchs. In 1891 they again moved, representing Ansonia in the Connecticut State League before the league folded.

That year the manager of the New York Gorhams, Ambrose Davis, signed some of the Cuban Giants players and formed a consolidated team called the Big Gorhams. Davis also attracted two other top players, George Stovey and Frank Grant, to assemble the best black team of the nineteenth century. But despite a phenomenal record of 100-4, the team failed at the box office and was forced to disband at the end of the season.

The next three seasons represented the lowest point in the history of black baseball, with the regrouped Cuban Giants being the only full-time black professional team. In 1896 the Giants defected to owner E. B. Lamar, Jr., to form a new ballclub called the Cuban X-Giants, which would become the dominant black team during the remainder of the century and on into the early 1900s.

Meanwhile, in the Midwest, black baseball was thriving and seemed ready to support a professional team. Chicago, long the hub of black baseball in the region, had seen its first team, the Unions, organized in 1887. After competing as a strong amateur team for nearly a decade, the Unions turned professional in 1896.

In the professional ranks another midwestern team, the Page Fence Giants, excelled during the mid-1890s. Organized in 1894 by Bud Fowler and Grant "Home Run" Johnson, the team was based in Adrian, Michigan, and featured Fowler as playing manager and Johnson as captain. Fowler selected his players based on ability and character. Among his original dozen players, none used alcohol and only two used tobacco. Five were college graduates.

J. Wallace Page, a Civil War veteran and founder of the Page Woven Wire Fence Company, sponsored the all-black ballclub as a promotional stunt. The team traveled by railroad throughout the United States and Canada in a special coach with the company's name painted on the side.

The Page Fence Giants combined baseball and show business. After their arrival in a town, the team, dressed in uniforms and fire hats, paraded from the railroad station to the ballpark on bicycles, which were quite the rage in the 1890s. During the actual game, the players would entertain fans with an assortment of comedic antics, including a "noisy coaching" routine.

But the Page Fence Giants were more than entertainers; they were an outstanding baseball team as well. The club played its first game on April 9, 1895, and with manager Gus Parsons at the helm, went on to compile an impressive record of 118 wins, 36 losses, and 2 ties in its first season. The next year an even-stronger Page Fence team defeated the Cuban Giants nine games to six in a challenge series for the Colored Championship. In 1897 they achieved a 125-12 mark, including 82 straight victories. But despite their success on the diamond, the team suffered financial difficulties, and in 1898 the club dissolved.

Most of the players moved to the Chicago Columbia Giants in 1899, enabling the club to defeat the more established Chicago Unions in a play-off for the western title. That year, the Cuban X-Giants won in the East, and a championship series was arranged between the two teams to close out the century. The X-Giants prevailed, winning 9 of 14 games to claim the Colored Championship.

While all-black teams were growing in popularity, there were few black players in organized—that is to say, league—baseball during the last five years of the century. In isolated cases black players still found work, but as the century drew to a close, the handwriting was on the wall. In 1898 the Celeron Acme Giants, a team of young and inexperienced black players in an obscure league, became the last black professional team in organized baseball at any level.

In 1899 one black player, Bill Galloway, appeared in five games in the Canadian League. This marked the last time a black player appeared alongside whites in organized baseball until Jackie Robinson joined the Montreal Royals, the Brooklyn Dodgers' farm club, in 1946. The next century would start with two parallel baseball worlds, separated by a color line.

2

A New Century (1900–1909)

Charlie Grant, a veteran black ballplayer, was working as a bellhop at the Arkansas hotel where the Baltimore Orioles stayed during their 1901 spring training camp. After observing Grant in a pickup game of black hotel workers, Orioles manager John McGraw decided to sign the talented second baseman, telling the press that he was a full-blooded Cherokee named Chief Charlie Tokohama. The deception unraveled when Grant was recognized by fans in Chicago, where he had starred the previous year, before opening day.

ALTHOUGH THERE WERE no known African-American players in organized professional baseball at the turn of the century, rumors persisted that the major leagues contained a few blacks who had managed to pass themselves off as white or Cuban, and speculation that a major league franchise would soon openly sign top black players was sometimes voiced. However, the mind-set of the times made an integrated league highly unlikely. Racism permeated American society, and the concept of "separate but equal" treatment for whites and blacks was widely accepted. The unwritten practice of excluding black players from organized baseball was so firmly entrenched that it carried the weight of official policy.

Nevertheless, John McGraw, who would later gain fame as the manager of the New York Giants, attempted to circumvent this policy in the first years of the century. In 1901 McGraw was manager of the Baltimore Orioles in the newly organized American League. The Orioles were holding their spring training in Hot Springs, Arkansas, and were staying at the Eastland Hotel. One day McGraw observed some black bellhops playing baseball on the hotel grounds and was impressed by the skills of one of the players. The man—whose name, McGraw learned, was Charlie Grant—was a seasoned player, with five years of professional experience on top black teams. In need of quality ballplayers, McGraw decided to sign Grant, telling the press that the light-skinned second baseman was a full-blooded Cherokee named Chief Charlie Tokohama.

Grant practiced with the Orioles throughout the spring and accompanied the team north to Chicago for an exhibition game against the White Sox. Unfortunately, Chicago was also the home of the Columbia Giants, the black team for which Grant had starred the previous year. The exuberant welcome "Chief Tokohama" received from the city's black fans doomed the charade, and White Sox owner Charlie Comiskey soon exposed McGraw's ruse. Grant was dropped from the roster before opening day, never to appear in a regular-season game with the Orioles.

While McGraw was trying to sneak a black player into the major leagues, Frank Leland was asserting himself as the top black baseball personality in the Midwest. Leland, a Chicago sportsman, had a varied career as a player, manager, and team owner, but he is best known as a pioneering organizer. He had moved to Chicago after graduating from Fisk University in Nashville, Tennessee, and was instrumental in organizing and developing five successful baseball teams in the city during his association with black baseball.

In 1900 the Columbia Giants and the Chicago Unions both claimed the Colored Championship in the Midwest. But there was no play-off, so the title remained in dispute. In 1901 Leland ended the disagreement by combining the two squads to form the Chicago Union Giants. He then appointed himself manager, and the team was recognized as a top team in the west.

In 1903 the Union Giants lost the western championship in a challenge play-off to a short-lived club from Algona, Iowa, called the Algona Brownies. But Leland's best teams were yet to come. In 1905 he formed a team that bore his name—the Leland Giants—and the club quickly earned a reputation as the top black team in the west. Leland made his biggest move toward achieving dominance in 1907 when he signed Rube Foster to manage the team. For Foster, this was a return to the city where he had started his professional career with Leland's Chicago Union Giants in 1902.

Rube Foster, who is called "the Father of the Negro Leagues," without question had the biggest influence on black baseball. The son of a Methodist minister, he was born September 17, 1879, in Calvert, Texas. After completing the eighth grade, he played semipro ball with the Waco Yellow Jackets. But not even Texas was big enough to hold the raw-boned youngster with the enormous baseball

The 1907 Chicago Leland Giants, who achieved a 48-game winning streak. Team founder and owner Frank Leland is wearing a suit; Rube Foster, the team's star pitcher and manager, is in the back row at the far right. The age of the photo is evidenced by the fading.

talent. Big, brash, and bold, Foster left the Lone Star State and took black baseball by storm.

In 1902 he chalked up 51 victories for the Leland Giants, including a win over the great white pitcher Rube Waddell, which earned him his nickname. After just one year with Leland, Foster left Chicago and moved east to join the Cuban X-Giants, the reigning eastern champions.

That year Dan McClellan, the X-Giants' ace left-hander, pitched the first perfect game in black baseball history. The victim of his sterling work was York (Pennsylvania) of the Tri-State League. Despite his great feat, McClellan had to take a backseat to Foster. The big Texan was credited with an astounding 54-1 record for the season.

At the end of the season the Philadelphia Giants rose up to challenge the Cuban X-Giants for the eastern title. Foster, however, had other ideas. In the play-off, he capped his remarkable season by winning four games to give the Cuban X-Giants the championship.

The following season the same teams met in a play-off and the same pitcher was the star. But this time the Philadelphia Giants emerged victorious, as Foster, who had joined the club in the off-season, hurled two victories against his former teammates to wrap up the three-game series. Clearly, Rube Foster was the dominant force in the game.

The Philadelphia Giants had been organized in 1902 by Sol White, a former star baseball player, and H. Walter Schlichter, a white sportswriter. After White enticed Rube Foster to Philadelphia, they became the best team in black baseball. For the next two years, with Foster as their ace hurler, the Giants added two more championships to give them three titles in a row. Even after Foster left the team, the Giants continued their winning ways and added a fourth straight title in 1907. Their highest winning percentage (.848) came in 1905, when

they compiled a 134-21-3 mark. In 1907, while managing the team, White wrote *Sol White's Official Base Ball Guide*, which helped preserve the history of the early years of black baseball.

After leaving the Philadelphia Giants because of a salary dispute, Foster returned to Chicago and began his managerial career at the helm of the Leland Giants. Under Foster's command, the team immediately developed a winning tradition and put together a 48-game winning streak. By the end of the decade the Leland Giants, with Rube Foster as their manager and star pitcher, were ready to challenge any team, white or black.

In August of 1909 the Lelands played in a five-game challenge series for the western championship. Their opponents were the St. Paul Gophers, an upstart club managed by Chappie Johnson, who had been a teammate of Foster's the previous winter in a Cuban league. The Gophers

The Philadelphia Giants, paced by the overpowering pitching of Rube Foster (seated, second from right), won black championships in 1905 and 1906.

had been improving steadily over the course of the season, and an extensive recruiting program in the South had resulted in a new infusion of talent, making St. Paul the only black team worthy of challenging Foster's club for the top spot.

While the Gophers were coming on strong, the Lelands' fortunes had taken a turn for the worse. In mid-July Foster had sustained a broken leg in the first inning of a game against the Cuban Stars. Though he had left the field unaided, an examination had revealed that a small bone in his left leg was broken, and he would be out of the lineup for six weeks. So if the Leland Giants were to win the western championship, they would have to do it without the strong arm of Rube Foster.

The opening game of the series was played on August 2 in St. Paul. A crowd of more than a thousand—including a sprinkling of white fans—attended. In a seesaw slugfest that was not decided until the 11th inning, the St. Paul Gophers won on a three-run homer just inside the foul pole. With crowds ranging from 800 to 1,500 enthusiastic fans, the Lelands won two of the next three games to knot the series going into the final game.

In that contest, the Lelands' ace left-hander Pat Dougherty pitched a no-hitter through seven innings and was cruising along with a 2-0 lead. In the eighth inning, however, the Gophers' bats came alive. After St. Paul loaded the bases on three singles, Eugene Milliner tripled to give the Gophers a 3-2 lead. "Steel Arm" Johnny Taylor, who had also won the series opener, retired the Lelands in the ninth to give the Gophers the western championship. This was the first time that a black team had ever won a series over the Leland Giants.

Most authorities agree that Foster's absence from the lineup was a decisive factor in the outcome of the hotly contested play-off. After he had recuperated from his injury, Foster was ready for a new

Chappie Johnson, manager of the St. Paul Gophers, who defeated the Leland Giants in a five-game challenge series in 1909 to claim the western championship of black baseball.

and bigger challenge. And he looked to the major leagues for the competition.

The Chicago Cubs had lost the National League pennant to Honus Wagner and the Pittsburgh Pirates and, for the first time in four years, found themselves sitting out the World Series. Rube Foster issued a challenge that would provide the Cubs with a fall series and possibly a fat paycheck: a three-game series pitting the best white team in Chicago against the best black team, to be played at the Cubs' home field. The Cubs accepted.

The first game, played on October 18, featured the Lelands' veteran hurler George Ball against the Cubs' ace and future Hall of Famer, Mordecai "Three Finger" Brown. The third inning produced an unforgettable play. After singling, the Lelands'

Joe Green promptly stole both second and third base. However, in sliding into third he broke his leg. When the ball got away from the third baseman, Green scrambled to his feet and hobbled toward home, only to be thrown out just a few steps from the plate. After the play was over, Green had to be carried off the field. The Lelands went on to lose the opener, largely because of a trio of errors.

The second game of the series was eagerly anticipated by fans and the media alike, in no small part because the well-known and colorful Rube Foster would be making his first appearance on the mound since suffering his midseason injury. As it turned out, few fans would soon forget the game's chaotic and bizarre conclusion.

Foster held the Cubs to two runs through eight innings and took the mound in the ninth with a 5-2 lead. With one out and fans streaming for the exits, the Cubs rallied to tie the score. Frank Schulte, the potential winning run, eventually reached third base with two outs. Because he had appeared to have the game under control, Foster did not have a relief pitcher warming up in the bullpen. So he walked over to the Lelands' bench to talk with Pat Dougherty about relieving him. The Cubs players crowded around the umpire, a man named Meyer, on the playing field near first base. They claimed that Foster was stalling. Several fans edged over the third base line and also got into the argument. As Foster stood with his back to the plate and the ball in his hand, Schulte sneaked home with the winning run.

Foster claimed he had called time out and demanded that Schulte be sent back to third, as both the Cubs players and spectators were on the field of play. Meyer, a white semipro umpire, ruled that he did not hear Foster call for time out and that the run counted. According to the press, even the rabid Cubs fans agreed that Schulte's stolen base was a "dirty steal," and the umpire had to be escort-ed from the field for his own protection.

There had been heavy betting on the game, and gamblers milled around the clubhouse, getting uglier by the minute. Finally, a spokesman climbed on a chair so he could be seen above the throng and shouted, "All bets are off!" That pronounce-ment soothed the mood of the crowd, but the bot-tom line was that Foster, a trickster himself, had been outfoxed.

The final game was probably the best contest of the series, but the Cubs emerged from the pitching duel with a 1-0 victory over the Lelands' Pat Dougherty. Although the Lelands had lost the three-game series, the games were closely contested, proving that black teams could be competitive with the best white teams.

The next season Rube Foster improved his ball-club and again challenged the Cubs. Having just won their fourth pennant in five years, however, the Cubs declined the invitation.

3

Free Agents and Independent Teams (1910–1919)

Two legendary pitchers, Smokey Joe Williams (left) and Cannonball Dick Redding, shake hands. Williams, who threw a blazing fastball, repeatedly bested white major league teams in exhibition games and dominated black baseball for more than 20 years. Redding once struck out 25 of 27 batters in a single game and chalked up 20 consecutive victories. Though the two men had been teammates on the Lincoln Giants club, in later years they became bitter rivals.

JOHN HENRY LLOYD, one of the premier black players of the 1910s, once remarked, "Wherever the money was, that's where I was." And wherever John Henry Lloyd was, it seemed, there the championship also was. This points to a big difference between black professional baseball and the white major leagues of the time: unlike the major league clubs, the black teams were independent. Without rules defining acceptable business practices—and a league structure to enforce them—nothing prevented owners from raiding other teams for talented players. In essence, every black player was a free agent.

In the earliest years of professional black baseball, the centers of activity were the eastern seaboard and the Midwest. New York City and Philadelphia attracted the top baseball talent in the East, while Chicago was the hotbed of baseball in the Midwest. As baseball gained popularity, the two geographical regions began to compete for top players. In addition to jumping from one region to another, players frequently jumped from one team to another within a region.

In the Midwest, Rube Foster and Frank Leland continued to be key figures in the development of black baseball. After making the Chicago Leland Giants into one of the top teams, they parted ways in 1910 and formed two separate teams.

Foster's team won the legal right to retain the name of Leland Giants for the 1910 season, though he changed the team's name to the American Giants in 1911. Leland's new team was called the Chicago Giants. Although both clubs continued through the decade and became charter members of the Negro National League in 1920, it was Foster's franchise that would dominate baseball in the Midwest. His 1910 ballclub—a virtual all-star team that featured John Henry Lloyd, Pete Hill, Bruce Petway, and Grant "Home Run" Johnson—finished with a record of 106-7. Foster considered this team the greatest baseball talent ever assembled, and it marked the beginning of a dynasty that would last until he departed from the game.

Because he felt that his team's success depended on having its own ballpark, Foster formed a business partnership with John Schorling, the son-in-law of White Sox owner Charles Comiskey. Through this arrangement the team played at the old Chicago White Sox Park.

As he gradually cut back on his playing time and concentrated on managing, Foster began to reshape the Chicago American Giants in his own image. He molded his players to fit his style of play—fast yet disciplined. He controlled every facet of the game and often signaled plays with the pipe that he always carried. And he ran the team with an iron hand. Once, a player ignored his signal to bunt and hit a triple instead. When the player returned to the dugout, Foster cracked him over the head with his pipe, declaring, "As long as I'm paying you, you'll do what I tell you to do."

The American Giants became the longest continuous franchise in the history of black baseball, finally disbanding in 1950. With one exception, the team won every recognized western championship during the first decade of its existence. That one exception came in 1916, when the Indianapolis ABCs took the title. The ABCs, the primary challenger to Foster's dominance, were managed by his rival, C. I. Taylor. These two giants of black baseball were both outstanding managers, and when their teams met on the baseball diamond, the fans were invariably treated to a hard-fought, closely contested ball game.

The intensity of the competition—and the seriousness with which fans followed the teams—was demonstrated during one such encounter in 1915. With the two teams locked in a close contest (and heavy betting on the outcome), Pete Hill, Foster's star center fielder and captain, got into an argument with the umpire, who promptly pulled a gun and hit Hill in the nose. This provoked a riot, and the game was forfeited to the ABCs. Though the two teams remained evenly matched, implacable rivals throughout the season, the American Giants managed to win the play-off for the championship.

The next season the two teams had a play-off rematch, and this time the ABCs emerged with the title. Previously the ABCs had been a franchise of lesser distinction. But in 1914 owner Thomas Bowser and manager C. I. Taylor had stocked the team with players of major league caliber, and the team quickly became one of the best in black baseball. Following the 1915 season, however, a split developed between Bowser and Taylor, and the 1916 season opened with two ABC teams. Taylor's team ultimately retained the quality players who formed the nucleus of his championship squad, and Bowser's team dropped into obscurity.

The ABCs were a family affair, with C. I. Taylor tapping several of his brothers to play for him. Steel Arm Johnny was a pitcher, Candy Jim an infielder. But the best ballplayer in the family was Ben, the

Hall of Famer John Henry Lloyd, considered baseball's best shortstop—black or white—between 1910 and 1920, went on to have a distinguished career as a manager.

youngest brother, who began his career as a left-handed pitcher but quickly became the premier first baseman of his era. In later years, Ben would teach future Hall of Famer Buck Leonard the art of playing first base.

Another budding superstar, Oscar Charleston, also began his baseball career as a left-handed pitcher with the ABCs and went on to excel at another position. For Charleston that position was center field, and before his career had ended, some observers believed he was the best center fielder in all of baseball—better even than Ty Cobb and Tris Speaker.

C. I. Taylor was a master at teaching the game of baseball and developing young talent. Unfortunately for him, many of the ballplayers he developed ended up starring on Rube Foster's teams. As one reporter observed, "C. I. trains 'em and Rube signs 'em."

The player who most epitomized Rube Foster's style of play was Pete Hill, another outfielder frequently mentioned as the equal of Cobb or Speaker. Hill, the captain of the American Giants, was a complete ballplayer. A left-handed batter, he hit with amazing consistency and good power and also excelled at bunting for base hits. In center field he had excellent range, fielded flawlessly, and had a deadly arm. And on the base paths his outstanding speed and nervy baserunning upset many a pitcher and infielder, just as Jackie Robinson would do over a quarter century later.

Foster's top pitchers throughout much of the 1910s were Frank Wickware and Richard Whitworth, while C. I. Taylor's ABCs featured Dizzy Dismukes. During the middle of the decade, when the two teams were battling for the championship, both managers coveted a tall, slender left-hander named John Donaldson. But neither Foster nor Taylor succeeded in signing him. Donaldson's best years were spent with the All Nations team, a unique club composed of players from assorted ethnic backgrounds (black, white, American Indian, Asian, and Hispanic). The team was organized and owned by J. L. Wilkinson, a white businessman from Kansas City, and J. E. Gall. The All Nations team toured the Midwest until most of its top players were drafted for service in World War I, and the club disbanded in 1918.

While Foster's American Giants were dominating the Midwest, there was a changing of the guard in the East. After a disagreement with owner Walter Schlichter, Philadelphia Giants manager Sol White left to form his own team. But unlike Frank Leland and Rube Foster, who both prospered after their split, neither White nor Schlichter was able to maintain a quality ballclub.

In 1916, the Indianapolis ABCs upset Rube Foster's Chicago American Giants for the western championship of black baseball. Owned and managed by C. I. Taylor, the ABCs featured three of Taylor's brothers: Steel Arm Johnny, a pitcher; Candy Jim, an infielder; and Ben, a first baseman.

This left the field open for a new team. The Lincoln Giants were organized in New York by Jess McMahon, a white businessman and sports promoter, and immediately became the best team in the East, winning three consecutive titles from 1911 to 1913. The team featured John Henry Lloyd (who had jumped from Foster's team), Cyclone Joe Williams, Cannonball Dick Redding, Louis Santop, and Spot Poles. All of these players were superstars and would have excelled in the major leagues.

John Henry Lloyd was the decade's best shortstop—black or white—supplanting Honus Wagner, who had passed his prime. Wagner considered it an honor to be compared with Lloyd, who, like the Pittsburgh Pirates great, would later be enshrined in the Hall of Fame.

Lloyd was a smart player and served as playing manager on the team in 1912 and 1913. In the final year of the team's championship "threepeat," the Lincoln Giants easily defeated Rube Foster's Chicago American Giants in a play-off for the Colored Championship. For the rest of the decade, Lloyd jumped back and forth between the east and the west.

Another star for the Lincolns was catcher Louis Santop, the premier slugger of the dead-ball era. (In the early days of baseball, the balls used were said to be "dead"—that is, they lacked springiness and were therefore difficult to hit far.) A big Texan with a cannonlike arm, Santop earned the nickname "Big Bertha," after the Germans' World War I long-range artillery piece. Standing at home plate, he could throw a ball over the center field fence, but he could hit a ball even farther. Santop's ability to "call his shots"—as Babe Ruth was later said to have done in one of baseball's most fabled moments—made him a crowd favorite. In his prime, he was the biggest drawing card in black baseball and also the highest-paid player, earning $500 a month. Though

Among the stars on the 1911 Lincoln Giants team were center fielder Spot Poles (back row, far right), shortstop John Henry Lloyd (middle row, center), and catcher Louis Santop (middle row, far right).

he changed teams frequently, Santop played primarily with teams based in New York. In addition to the Lincoln Giants, these teams included the Lincoln Stars and the Brooklyn Royal Giants. He joined Ed Bolden's Hilldale club in 1917 but entered the U.S. Navy during World War I and missed most of the next two seasons. By the time he returned to Hilldale, a new decade and a new baseball era had begun. The dead-ball era was over, and home runs were an even more important aspect of the game.

While Santop furnished the power for the Lincolns, Spot Poles provided the speed. The top outfielder in the east, Poles rivaled the Chicago American Giants' Pete Hill, who was the best in the west. Poles was an ideal lead-off batter, and in 1911, his first year with the Lincoln Giants, he stole 41 bases

Hilldale, which played out of Darby, Pennsylvania, won the first three Eastern Colored League championships (1923-25). Owner Ed Bolden (far right) was the man most responsible for the league's founding.

in only 60 games. His speed is compared with that of another great center fielder, James "Cool Papa" Bell, who starred in the Negro leagues some years later.

Poles stayed with the Lincoln Giants through-out most of his career but joined the Hilldale club in 1918. Like Santop, his baseball career was inter-rupted by Word War I. Poles joined the infantry, advanced to the rank of sergeant, and served with distinction, earning five battle stars and a Purple Heart for his combat service in France. He was sometimes called "the black Ty Cobb," and New York Giants manager John McGraw listed Poles as one of the black players he would pick for the major leagues if the color line did not exist.

In the dead-ball era of baseball, pitching was dominant, and the Lincoln Giants at one time featured two of the top pitchers of the decade: Cannonball Dick Redding and Cyclone Joe Williams. Redding was credited with 30 no-hitters in his career, but many were against semipro teams. He began his career in 1911 with the Philadelphia Giants. In July, the rookie moved to the Lincoln Giants for the remainder of the year and won 17 straight games. The following year he fanned 25 of 27 batters in one game. In 1915, after moving to the Lincoln Stars, he chalked up 20 straight victories before losing a game. A hard worker with exceptional stamina, he often pitched doubleheaders two or three days in succession.

Redding joined the Chicago American Giants in 1917 and pitched Rube Foster's team to a championship before entering the army during World War I. After combat duty in France, he returned to the United States and soon reestablished himself in the east with the Brooklyn Royal Giants.

As formidable as Redding was on the mound, the distinction of being the greatest pitcher of the first half-century of black baseball goes to Cyclone Joe (later called Smokey Joe) Williams. Williams earned his nickname because his fastball was described as moving like a pebble tossed by a cyclone.

Williams excelled when playing white major league teams, compiling a 20-7 lifetime record in exhibition games against major leaguers. Ty Cobb, never known for his racial tolerance, considered Williams to be a "sure 30-game winner" if he could pitch in the majors. In 1912 he struck out nine batters en route to a 6-0 shutout of the New York Giants. A year later, with Grover Cleveland Alexander opposing him on the mound, he led the Lincolns to a 9-2 upset win over the Philadelphia Phillies. These and other games stimulated arguments as to who had the better teams—black baseball or the white major leagues.

Years later the tall, hard-throwing right-hander would move to the steel city of Pittsburgh and become better known as Smokey Joe Williams. The blazing fastball that earned him his nicknames made him a dominant force in black baseball for more than 20 years. In a 1952 *Pittsburgh Courier* poll, Williams was rated above the legendary Satchel Paige as the all-time greatest black pitcher.

In 1914, after three years of eastern dominance with the Lincoln Giants, the McMahon brothers formed the Lincoln Stars, a rival team that was also based in New York. The Stars lasted for three seasons and won the eastern championship during their last two (1915 and 1916), but the McMahon brothers had other sporting interests and ended their direct involvement with black baseball.

As the end of the decade approached, two more teams came into prominence in the east when the Bacharach Giants and Hilldale began recruiting top ballplayers for their clubs. The Hilldale team, based in Darby, Pennsylvania, began as a boys' team in 1910 but went pro in 1916. They improved quickly and by 1918 were competitive with any team in the east.

The Bacharachs were organized to provide an activity to keep black youths off the boardwalk in Atlantic City, New Jersey. The team had originated in Jacksonville, Florida, as the Duval Giants and, in 1916, moved intact to Atlantic City. The team was bankrolled by two black Atlantic City politicians, and assumed the team name in honor of the city's mayor, Harry Bacharach.

As the decade came to a close, Joe Williams and Dick Redding continued to reign as the two top attractions in the east. In 1919 the two star fastballers faced each other on opening day, with Williams tossing a no-hitter to give the Lincoln Giants a win over the Royal Giants. As the two stars, who were once teammates, vied for supremacy, they became involved in a bitter feud. According to a New York newspaper, Redding made "no secret of his belief that he was Joe Williams' master," and the two men refused to shake hands for photographers after a game.

In the west, the Detroit Stars challenged Foster's American Giants for dominance. Playing under the ownership of Rube Foster's friend Tenny Blount, the Stars fielded a strong team in their first season, with Pete Hill at the helm. During his long tenure with Foster's ballclub, Hill had served his managerial apprenticeship. In 1919 he faced his mentor in a challenge series. Hill connected with his 19th homer of the season to lead the Stars to victory over his ex-teammates. Though disappointed by the defeat, Rube Foster had bigger things in mind for the future.

4

The Early Leagues (1920–1931)

Rube Foster, "the Father of the Negro Leagues." In 1920, largely by the strength of his indomitable personality, Foster managed to organize the first black professional baseball league, the Negro National League. As president of the league, which initially contained eight teams, he proved a tireless, visionary, and, at times, dictatorial leader.

RUBE FOSTER HAD already made his mark as a player, manager, and club executive. Now he was ready to take the biggest step in his long career. Foster dreamed of black players and black teams playing in the major leagues. But before this dream could become a reality, he believed, a quality black league patterned after the white major leagues but free from the controlling influences of white promoters would have to be established. And in order for such a league to succeed, Foster felt, two conditions would have to be met. First, each team would need to have access to its own ballpark. Second, and even more important, there would have to be parity within the league; if one or two teams dominated the others, fans would quickly lose interest.

As the new decade started, Foster moved to lay the groundwork for his plan. Recognizing the power of the press to drum up support for his endeavor, he drafted an article for the *Chicago Defender*, the Midwest's most influential black newspaper. In it he wrote, "We cannot get along without organization. Many colored men with money have begged us to get into the game, but they want it patterned after the way leagues are conducted." Black baseball as it existed, Foster asserted, was plagued by distrust, the result of such unethical practices as owners' tampering with players from other teams. Foster insisted that an agreement between club owners to respect the rights of other owners would solve this problem. But talk of such an agreement made the players leery, for they feared that an end to free agency would restrict their income. On the contrary, Foster argued, because salaries were ultimately limited by the gate receipts, bigger ballparks would mean bigger crowds and bigger paychecks for everyone.

Foster's efforts paid off. On February 13, 1920, the National Association of Colored Professional Baseball Clubs (more commonly known as the Negro National League) was organized during a meeting at the YMCA in Kansas City, Missouri. The league constitution was written by a group of sportswriters who worked through the night and into the next morning framing the black baseball "bill of rights." The document was then amended, approved, and signed by the representatives of the teams present at the conference—marking the beginning of the Negro leagues.

As the moving force in founding the league, Rube Foster was elected its president; his longtime rival, C. I. Taylor, served as vice president. Each franchise was required to post a $500 fee, which bound it to the league and its constitution. Teams forming the league were the Chicago American Giants, Indianapolis ABCs, Detroit Stars, Kansas City Monarchs, St. Louis Giants, Chicago Giants, Dayton Marcos, and Cuban Stars.

Foster realized that star players and closely contested games would be the key to attracting large crowds to the ballparks. To achieve this, he dictated the relocation of selected players to ensure that each team would have its share of stars. And, setting a good example, he parted with two of his top players.

Raleigh "Biz" Mackey, switch-hitting slugger for the Hilldale club. Though known primarily as a catcher, Mackey could play any position.

The first Negro National League game, played on May 2, 1920, saw Foster's Chicago American Giants drop a 4-2 contest to the Indianapolis ABCs. But this did not portend difficult times for Foster's team: the American Giants soon began a winning streak and pulled far ahead in the standings.

Under Foster's guiding hand, the American Giants won the league's first three pennants. The team's biggest stars were Cristobal Torriente, Bingo DeMoss, and Dave Brown. Torriente, flanked by Jimmy Lyons and Jelly Gardner, formed one of the fastest outfields of all time. In addition to being speedy, he was also a power hitter—the only one in Foster's lineup. C. I. Taylor said of the stocky left-hander, "There walks a ballclub." During the winter of 1920, he played against the touring New York Giants in Cuba. The Giants had added Babe Ruth to their roster for the 19-game series, and Torriente outhit and outhomered the great Sultan of Swat. Had it not been for the coarse texture of his hair, New York would have signed the light-skinned Cuban to play in the major leagues.

DeMoss, a slick second baseman who excelled at turning the double play and fit perfectly into the

American Giants mold, was the team captain. Before Foster lured him to Chicago, he had played with C. I. Taylor's Indianapolis ABCs.

Brown had encountered trouble with the law in Texas. Foster interceded and brought him to Chicago to anchor his pitching staff. The left-hander proved to be not only the ace of the staff but also the most effective pitcher in the entire league.

Foster's long-range goal had been to expand his league to include franchises in the larger cities along the eastern seaboard. However, the success of the Negro National League encouraged teams in the East to organize a separate league for themselves. Hilldale owner Ed Bolden was the driving force in forming the Eastern Colored League in 1923. In addition to his own club, the league included the Bacharach Giants, Baltimore Black Sox, New York Lincoln Giants, Brooklyn Royal Giants, and Cuban Stars. The next year the Harrisburg Giants were added, and the franchise became a league mainstay.

In contrast to the huge, flamboyant Rube Foster, Bolden was a small, shy, and modest man who preferred working in the background. But like Foster, Bolden owned the team that initially dominated the league he formed. His Hilldale club won the first three Eastern Colored League championships, from 1923 to 1925.

Bolden's league was responsible for player raids on the more established Negro National League. The Lincoln Giants started this trend in January of 1923 by signing Dave Brown, Rube Foster's star pitcher. (A year later Brown would disappear after killing a man in a barroom fight.) As the raids continued, two Negro National League teams were eventually dissolved because they had lost so many players. Another early casualty of these raids was the impending Negro World Series between the two rival leagues, which was not played in the Eastern Colored League's inaugural season.

The loss of Brown weakened Rube Foster's team

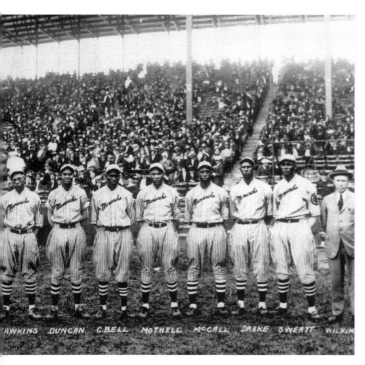

The Kansas City Monarchs, owned by J. L. Wilkinson (far right), at the first Negro World Series in 1924. The Monarchs, who had captured the Negro National League pennant, beat Hilldale, the Eastern Colored League champions, in the thrilling 10-game series.

considerably, and in 1923 the American Giants were dethroned by the hard-hitting Kansas City Monarchs, who took the first of their three consecutive Negro National League pennants. Owned by J. L. Wilkinson, a white businessman, and managed by Jose Mendez, the Monarchs featured pitcher-outfielder Wilbur "Bullet" Rogan and several other former stars of the U.S. Army's black 25th Infantry Regiment ballclub. Rogan combined a great fastball and an exceptional curve to become the top pitcher in the league. When he wasn't doing mound duty, he was the starting center fielder and batting in the heart of the order. Hard-hitting shortstop Dobie Moore and slick-fielding second-baseman Newt Allen were other outstanding players for the new champions.

Meanwhile, Foster worked tirelessly to keep the league together. Franchises entered, faltered, and disbanded—only to be replaced with other ballclubs. But Foster also ruled with an iron hand. At one league meeting, for example, an owner went to sleep and woke up without a franchise. As his powers increased, some owners became dissatisfied with Foster's dictatorial manner.

Discord grew from his handling of the money generated by the league. Although he received no salary as president, Foster took 5 percent of the gate receipts of every league game and distributed the money without answering to anyone. In 1925, in the face of growing opposition to his unrestricted powers, Foster offered to resign. The other owners gave him a unanimous vote of confidence, but in reality his support was fading.

The sharp mind that Foster had exhibited in his prime was showing the effects of the tremendous pressure under which he had labored for many years. He railed against his own players, claiming they had "laid down on him." By this time a nervous breakdown was imminent. Sadly, Rube Foster,

James "Cool Papa" Bell, a
great hitter, is perhaps best
remembered for his awesome
speed. He was once clocked
circling the bases in 12 seconds, and some authorities
believe he was the fastest man
ever to play baseball.

once larger than life, fell victim to mental illness
and was placed in an institution for the remainder
of his days.

In his absence, his white business partner, John
M. Schorling, handled the American Giants' business affairs. On the field, third-baseman Dave
Malarcher, who had learned his baseball from Foster, assumed the managerial duties and promptly
guided the club to back-to-back pennants in 1926
and 1927.

Foster's influence was not limited to Malarcher's
managing. His younger half-brother, Willie Foster,
became the ace of the American Giants' pitching
staff and won many clutch games during each season. The younger Foster was the mirror image of his
older brother and is considered the greatest left-

The 1931 Homestead Grays, one of the greatest teams of all time, featured a roster that included Smokey Joe Williams (standing, center), Josh Gibson (to Williams' left, fourth from right), and Oscar Charleston (standing, second from right). Owner Cum Posey is standing at the far left.

hander in the history of the Negro leagues.

However, Rube Foster's executive abilities were missed. In the spring of 1928, Schorling alleged that he was being "squeezed out" by a conspiracy on the part of the other owners to keep the best clubs out of Chicago. He sold the ballclub to William E. Trimble, a white florist, who also encountered difficulties.

The Kansas City Monarchs added another pennant in 1929 behind the hurling of Chet Brewer, while the St. Louis Stars won the league's last two pennants (1930 and 1931). These teams featured the speedy center fielder James "Cool Papa" Bell, superstar shortstop Willie "Devil" Wells, and slugging first baseman George "Mule" Suttles. In addition to being a perennial .300 hitter, Cool Papa Bell may have been the fastest baseball player ever. The great black pitcher Satchel Paige said that he could "switch the lights off and get into bed before the room got dark." Stories about Bell's speed abound.

The speedster would go from first to third on a bunt, could score from second base on a sacrifice fly, and was once clocked circling the bases in 12 seconds. Cool Papa Bell eventually ran his way into the Hall of Fame.

Wells was one of the greatest shortstops of all time, black or white. A fiery competitor, he excelled at all facets of the game. In the field he had a wide range, sure hands, and an accurate arm. Opponents would say, "Don't hit the ball to short-stop because the Devil's playing out there today." On the bases he ran aggressively with spikes high, like Ty Cobb. At the plate he hit for high averages and with good power. At different times during his years with the St. Louis Stars, he led the league in batting average, home runs, and stolen bases.

The hulking Suttles was a slugging first base-man–outfielder who could hit the ball as far as any-one. When he came up to bat, the crowd would yell, "Kick, Mule!" to encourage him to "kick" one of his towering homers out of the ballpark.

Another home run hitter of this era was Turkey Stearnes, who batted the Detroit Stars to the sec-ond-half title of the split season in 1930. But Detroit's challenge for the pennant fell short when they dropped a play-off to the St. Louis Stars, who had captured the first-half title.

Over in the Eastern Colored League, Hilldale, under manager John Henry Lloyd, had won the league's first pennant in 1923. But despite his suc-cess, Lloyd was fired, and the plucky little second baseman Frank Warfield took the helm of the ball-club. Hilldale's roster included such talented per-formers as Judy Johnson, Biz Mackey, Clint Thomas, and Nip Winters.

Johnson, a future Hall of Famer, was regarded as the best black third baseman of his era. He was a standout both in the field and at the plate. In later years he played with the Homestead Grays and the

Pittsburgh Crawfords.

Mackey, a switch-hitter, batted cleanup and shone in the clutch. But he is best known for his defensive skills and rifle arm. A superlative catcher, he later became Roy Campanella's mentor, and Campanella rated Mackey as his superior in every phase of the game except home run power.

Thomas, a star outfielder, was nicknamed "Hawk" because of his sharp eye at the plate and his ability to catch anything hit in his direction. In later years he starred with the New York Black Yankees.

Winters, a tall left-hander, was Hilldale's ace hurler and earned recognition as the best pitcher in the history of the Eastern Colored League. With this depth of talent on the team, Warfield promptly guided Hilldale to another two consecutive pennants. By then the two rival leagues had made peace, and each of these seasons was followed by a Negro World Series.

The first Negro World Series, played in 1924, pitted the Negro National League champion Kansas City Monarchs and Hilldale, champions of the Eastern Colored League. Scheduled as a best-of-nine competition, the series was a thrilling struggle that actually required 10 games to decide, as one game ended in a tie. The Monarchs ultimately prevailed to become the first Negro World Champions.

The next season's World Series featured a rematch between the two teams. However, this year the Monarchs were forced to play without their star pitcher, Wilbur "Bullet" Rogan, who was injured shortly before the first game. Rogan's absence proved decisive, and Hilldale won the series.

Only two more World Series were played between these two leagues. In 1926 and 1927, with manager Dave Malarcher at the reins, the Chicago American Giants won both the Negro National League flag and the Negro World Series. Each time they faced the Eastern Colored League's Bacharach Giants, under the leadership of playing manager Dick Lundy, and each year Willie Foster, the ace of the Chicago staff, pitched the clinching victory.

Although the Bacharachs lost both titles, they had the distinction of having a no-hitter in each series. Red Grier hurled the first one in 1926 and Luther Farrell added another the following year, although that game was called in the seventh inning because of darkness.

In 1927 the Eastern Colored League's prime mover, Ed Bolden—like his counterpart Rube Foster before him—suffered a nervous breakdown. Without his leadership, the league folded the following spring. A replacement league called the American Negro League—which was essentially the same league with a new name—operated for the 1929 season before also folding. The Baltimore Black Sox won the pennant in the league's only year of existence. The Black Sox featured ace right-hander Layman Yokely, slugging outfielder Rap Dixon, and an all-star infield consisting of Jud Wilson, Frank Warfield, Dick Lundy, and Oliver Marcelle.

Lundy, a superlative shortstop, had exceptional range and a strong arm. He was also a good hitter from both sides of the plate, and his polished play earned him the nickname "King Richard."

Marcelle, who played third base brilliantly, was called "The Ghost." Both he and his teammate Warfield were notoriously quick-tempered. Years later in Cuba, the two tangled in a fight in which Warfield bit off part of Marcelle's nose.

Jud Wilson also was a rugged adversary and fierce competitor. A pure hitter, he earned the nickname "Boojum" from the sound his line drives made when they hit the fence. Off the field he was likeable, but on the field he terrorized pitchers with his bat, and umpires with his tongue. Despite such combustible temperaments, the Black Sox easily won the 1929 pennant.

There was no World Series that year, and in 1930 the eastern teams returned to independent play. However, history was made when the Kansas City Monarchs and the Homestead Grays played a night game in Pittsburgh on August 2. But the Monarchs' portable lighting system, which helped pioneer night baseball, was not the only thing noteworthy about the contest. The game also included sensational performances by the opposing pitchers, Smokey Joe Williams and Chet Brewer. Brewer fanned 19 while allowing only four hits. Williams did even better, throwing a one-hitter and fanning 27 to give the Grays a 1-0 victory in the 12-inning marathon.

Manager John Henry Lloyd's 1930 Lincoln Giants fielded one of the strongest teams in their history. At midseason, behind the hitting of Chino Smith and John Beckwith, they looked unstoppable. But late in the season the Homestead Grays acquired a young catcher named Josh Gibson. The husky teenager, who was pressed into service behind the plate when veteran catcher Buck Ewing split a finger, made an immediate impact. Gibson, who would become the greatest slugger in the history of black baseball, powered the Grays to victory over the Lincoln Giants in a play-off for the eastern championship.

The next year, while playing on one of the greatest teams ever assembled—a team that included sluggers Oscar Charleston and Jud Wilson and pitchers Smokey Joe Williams and Lefty Williams—Gibson was credited with 75 home runs, and the Grays captured another championship.

The 1931 season was significant for another reason. For the first time in 30 years, Rube Foster was not a part of big-time black baseball. Two weeks before Christmas in 1930, the man recognized as the

Father of the Negro Leagues died in Kankakee, Illinois. Fans and admirers lined up for three days to view the casket. From the day he had arrived on the baseball scene until his death, Foster had stood astride the world of black baseball like a colossus.

5

Troubled Waters (1932–1936)

WHEN HE FOUNDED the Negro National League, Rube Foster had said, "We are the ship, all else is the sea." When Foster passed away in 1930, the ship had lost its rudder as well as its captain. Within a year of his death, the league also had expired, a victim of the Great Depression and the loss of the visionary leadership that Foster had provided.

With the collapse of the Negro National League, black baseball was thrown into a state of chaos. As their teams disbanded, a multitude of good players were suddenly out of work. The clubs that struggled to continue during this difficult period had their pick from among the glut of instant free agents.

Stepping into the breach was Cum Posey, owner of the Homestead Grays. In an effort to salvage ailing franchises all across the country, Posey organized the East-West League. Unfortunately, the league cities were widely scattered, which made traveling expenses too high for the league to succeed. By midseason the East-West League had folded, and the teams that survived returned to playing independent schedules that did not require long and expensive trips.

Josh Gibson during his early days with the Pittsburgh Crawfords. In addition to being the Negro leagues' greatest slugger, Gibson was a superlative catcher. Hall of Fame pitcher Walter Johnson once said of him, "[H]e catches so easy he might as well be in a rocking chair."

Another beneficiary of the free-agent glut was the Negro Southern League, which had been operating as a minor league. With the influx of more skilled players from northern cities, where the disbanding teams were located, the league acquired major league status in 1932. However, this status proved short lived.

In 1933 two team owners, Gus Greenlee and Tom Wilson, organized a new Negro National League. The two also hit on another idea that would be critical to the success of the Negro leagues: they arranged the first black all-star game, patterned after major league baseball's midseason classic. This event, which pitted the best players in the east against the best players in the west, was called the East-West Game. The results exceeded everyone's expectations—the game proved to be the biggest black sporting attraction ever staged. Thereafter, the East-West Game became an annual classic and continued to be the most popular and profitable venture in black baseball.

Twenty thousand fans from across the country converged on Comiskey Park for the inaugural game in 1933. They saw Willie Foster, Rube Foster's younger half-brother, pitch the full nine innings to give the West an 11-7 victory. The only thing missing from the historic game was Satchel Paige.

LeRoy Robert Paige was arguably the best pitcher in baseball, black or white, and wherever he went he attracted attention. The long, lanky hurler used a blazing fastball, a nimble wit, and a colorful personality to become a legend in his own time. Batters who faced Paige said that his fastball seemed to get smaller as it approached the plate. Some said it appeared to be the size of a half dollar, while others said it looked no bigger than a pea or a BB. Biz Mackey, who caught Paige, even declared that once Satchel threw the ball so hard that it disappeared before it reached his mitt—an example of the kind

of exaggerated tales everyone liked to tell about Paige's legendary fastball.

Paige had names for his pitches, including the "bee-ball," "jump-ball," "trouble ball," and "long-ball." His favorite, the "hesitation pitch," would eventually be outlawed when he joined the major leagues.

He was the ultimate showman. To attract a crowd, he often would warm up by using a chewing-gum wrapper or a matchbox for home plate. Once the game started, he had other tricks up his sleeve. On many occasions, for example, Paige would pull in his outfielders to sit behind the mound while he struck out the side. In exhibition games, he some-times guaranteed that he would strike out the first nine batters he faced, and he usually did. Some fans who witnessed these exhibitions thought Paige was bragging. "If you can do it," he asserted, "it ain't bragging." And there were many major leaguers who agreed that he wasn't bragging. Joe DiMaggio

Satchel Paige, perhaps the greatest African-American pitcher of all time, played for numerous teams. In 1942, when this photo was taken, he starred for the Kansas City Monarchs. Here he is shown warming up before a game in Yankee Stadium with the New York Cuban Giants.

and Babe Herman, both of whom played winter ball against him, claimed that Paige was the toughest pitcher they had ever faced.

Once, Paige pitched a no-hitter against the Homestead Grays in Pittsburgh and proceeded to Chicago, where he shut out the Chicago American Giants in 12 innings *on the same day.* Another time, as his teammates watched dumbfounded, he intentionally walked two batters in the ninth inning of a close game so he could pitch to his former teammate Josh Gibson, the most feared hitter in the Negro leagues, who believed that he, not Paige, was the best player around. "I'm gonna throw you some fastballs," Paige called from the mound. Then, after whizzing two fastballs past Gibson, Paige declared,

"I'm gonna throw a pea at your knee," which he did, fanning the slugger on three pitches.

Satchel Paige began his professional career in 1926 with Chattanooga in the Negro Southern League. In 1927 he joined the Birmingham Black Barons in the more prestigious Negro National League and soon thereafter began playing year-round. He next signed with Tom Wilson, a prominent businessman from Nashville. Wilson's team began the 1931 season playing as the Cleveland Cubs, but before the season was over their star hurler had joined the Pittsburgh Crawfords. By 1933 Paige had become far and away the biggest gate attraction in black baseball, and his absence from the East-West Game had been a major disap-

The East-West Game, the Negro leagues' annual all-star classic, proved vital to the success of the reorganized leagues. This photo shows Willie Foster, the winning pitcher of the first East-West Game in 1933, being honored before the 1934 game at Comiskey Park in Chicago. Satchel Paige spoiled Foster's day, out-pitching the American Giants ace to give the East all-stars the victory.

pointment to fans. Those who yearned to see Paige face the best players in black baseball got their wish the next year, in the 1934 East-West Game. In an eagerly anticipated showdown, the Crawfords' ace dueled with the previous year's winning pitcher, Willie Foster. The game was scoreless when the two star hurlers entered for their respective teams, and Paige outshone Foster to walk away with a 1-0 win. Jud "Boojum" Wilson provided the margin of victory, knocking in Cool Papa Bell in the eighth inning for the game's only score. Paige fanned five in his stint to also outperform his eastern rival, Slim Jones, who had started the game for the East squad and struck out four.

Another memorable East-West Game, this one featuring a spectacular finish, was played in 1935. After nine innings, the game was tied 4-4, and then each team scored four times in the 10th to send the game into another extra inning. With the winning run on base in the bottom half of the 11th inning, slugger Josh Gibson—who already had four hits in the game—was intentionally walked to pitch to Mule Suttles. Suttles promptly foiled the West's strategy by cracking a three-run homer off Martin Dihigo to give the West an 11-8 victory.

But again, despite the exciting contest, the absence of Satchel Paige was a disappointment to many fans. Paige had jumped the league to play with a predominantly white semipro team in Bismarck, North Dakota. However, he returned the next year and combined with Leroy Matlock and Bill Byrd to pitch the East to an easy 10-2 win that evened the all-star games at two wins apiece.

During this time, the best team in black baseball was the Pittsburgh Crawfords. The team had been assembled by Gus Greenlee, a businessman, politician, and sportsman better known as "Big Red," who had also been instrumental in resurrecting the Negro National League. In addition to owning the

Crawfords, Greenlee owned a stable of boxers, including the first black light-heavyweight champion, John Henry Louis.

When Greenlee bought the team, the Crawfords were a semipro club consisting mostly of young players. But he soon captured the attention of fans—and made the Crawfords a powerhouse—by signing such established stars as Satchel Paige, Josh Gibson, and Oscar Charleston. In 1932 he built Greenlee Field, the only black-owned ballpark in the east, as his home park, and from that year until 1936 the Crawfords were considered "the Yankees of the Negro leagues."

Satchel Paige was, of course, the team's most famous star. But his battery mate, catcher Josh Gibson, won fame with his awesome bat. Just as Babe Ruth was idolized by white children, Gibson earned the admiration of black youngsters. In every ballpark they would point to a spot in the remotest part of the field and say, "Josh hit one over there." He once smacked a 580-foot drive that, it was estimated, would have traveled 700 feet had it not hit just below the top of Yankee Stadium. One player insists that Gibson actually hit a ball out of Yankee Stadium, but that has never been verified. Regardless, Gibson's homers have taken their place in baseball lore.

A tall tale popular at the time humorously illustrates his legendary power. At a game in Pittsburgh, the story goes, Gibson hit a mammoth home run that cleared the fence and sailed out of sight. The next day, in Philadelphia, a ball fell from the sky and landed in an outfielder's glove. The umpire promptly turned to Gibson and declared, "You're out yesterday in Pittsburgh!"

Josh Gibson first began playing baseball in 1927 with the Pleasant Valley Red Sox, a Pittsburgh sandlot team, before joining the Pittsburgh Crawfords later that season. At that time the Crawfords

Gus Greenlee bought a little-noticed semipro team, the Pittsburgh Crawfords, and transformed it into "the Yankees of the Negro leagues" by signing such talented players as Josh Gibson, Oscar Charleston, and Satchel Paige. Along with Nashville Elite Giants owner Tom Wilson, Greenlee also organized the new Negro National League after Rube Foster's original league had folded.

The East all-stars before the start of the 1939 East-West Game. Forty thousand fans jammed Comiskey Park and saw the West triumph, 4-2.

were still just a youth league team. While starring for the Crawfords, he attracted the attention of the Homestead Grays. After two years with the Grays, he returned to the Crawfords' fold in 1932 and stayed with Pittsburgh for the next five seasons. He is credited with 69 home runs in 1934 and 84 homers in 1936 to become a star among stars on the great Crawfords teams of that era.

Gus Greenlee was a driving force in black base-ball during his relatively short tenure as an owner and officer in the Negro leagues. Though he was a generous spender, in 1935 he and Satchel Paige had a salary dispute, and the star pitcher left in the midst of the season for the semipro team in Bismarck.

Another ex-Crawford, Ted "Double Duty" Radcliffe, had preceded Paige to Bismarck. Radcliffe had been playing with Pittsburgh when was given his nickname by the writer Damon Runyon. In a double-header at Yankee Stadium, Runyon watched him catch Paige in the first game and then take the mound to hurl a shutout in the second. The next day Runyon wrote that "it was worth the price of two admissions to see 'Double Duty' Radcliffe."

With Paige in North Dakota, the Crawfords turned to left-hander Leroy Matlock to assume the role of ace of the pitching staff, and Matlock responded by finishing the season without a loss. Even without the great Satchel Paige, the Crawfords won the championship by defeating the New York Cubans in a seven-game play-off. The 1935 Crawfords are considered by many experts to be the best black team of all time. The roster featured five future Hall of Famers—Josh Gibson, Oscar Charleston, Cool Papa Bell, Judy Johnson, and Satchel Paige (although he was absent most of the season).

The Crawfords won the second-half title the following year, but the play-off was not completed and no 1936 champion was recognized. In 1937 several top players, led by Satchel Paige and Josh Gibson, jumped to the Dominican Republic to play on dictator Rafael Trujillo's ballclub. The Crawfords never again regained their excellence from the five preceding seasons. After two poor seasons and a business reversal, Greenlee sold the team and tore down Greenlee Field.

The Crawfords were not the only good team during the Depression years. In the Midwest, the Chicago American Giants again fielded a top ballclub. After Rube Foster's death and the demise of the Negro National League, the franchise again rose to prominence as Cole's American Giants. The club won pennants in the Negro Southern League (1932) and the Negro National League (1933) behind the pitching of Willie Foster, the all-around play of Willie Wells, and the hitting of Mule Suttles, Walter "Steel Arm" Davis, and Alex Radcliffe.

Another team that challenged the Crawfords was the Philadelphia Stars, who captured the Negro National League banner in 1934 behind the pitching of a tall, hard-throwing left-hander, Slim Jones. "I faced both Slim Jones and Lefty Grove," Hall of Famer Buck Leonard says, "and of the two, I believe Slim Jones was a little bit faster." During his prime, Jones's fastball was compared with that of Satchel Paige.

On September 10, 1934, 30,000 fans at Yankee Stadium watched as Jones and Paige locked in a pitching duel that has been called the greatest game in the history of black baseball. The game was ended by darkness after nine complete innings with the score still a 1-1 stalemate. When the famous "shootout" was over, there was no consensus about who had performed best. Jones fanned nine and allowed only three hits. Paige struck out an even dozen but yielded six hits.

From that day on their careers went in different directions. Four years later, during the winter of 1938, Jones traded his overcoat for a bottle of whiskey, caught pneumonia, and died. Paige went on to a long career that eventually led to the major leagues and the Hall of Fame.

As Paige's career was soaring, another Hall of Famer's career was winding down. John Henry Lloyd retired from the Bacharach Giants in 1932 and settled in Atlantic City, where he assumed the role of elder statesman of black baseball. A rugged, aggressive competitor on the field, off the field he was easygoing. He neither drank nor smoked and rarely used coarse language. In his managerial capacity Lloyd was a master at instilling confidence in younger players.

He continued as manager and first baseman of sandlot teams until the age of 60. In his later years he became known affectionately as "Pop" and also served as Atlantic City's Little League commissioner. In 1949, in recognition of his involvement with youngsters, John Henry Lloyd Baseball Park was dedicated in his honor.

That was the year that Jackie Robinson was voted the National League's Most Valuable Player. Historians generally agree that Lloyd was superior to Robinson as a ballplayer, and in 1949 some people were saying that he had been born too soon. But at the dedication, Lloyd disagreed. "I do not consider that I was born at the wrong time," he said. "I felt it was the right time, for I had a chance to prove the ability of our race in this sport . . . [and] we have given the Negro a greater opportunity now to be accepted into the major leagues with other Americans."

6

Dynasties (1937–1946)

IN 1937 THE Negro American League was organized with teams in the Midwest and South. At the same time, the Negro National League restructured as an eastern league. For the next dozen seasons, the Negro leagues operated with two major leagues, just like the white major leagues.

During this time, two dynasties dominated their respective leagues. In the west, the Kansas City Monarchs won five of the first six Negro American League pennants before World War II interrupted their string. Once their best players returned from military service, they added a sixth pennant in 1946. In the east, the Homestead Grays dominated the Negro National League, winning nine straight pennants (1937–1945).

The man who built the Grays' dynasty was Cum Posey. Born in Homestead, Pennsylvania, Posey excelled at sports. In college he was best known for his basketball skills, but he also had a talent for baseball. After joining the Grays as a player in 1912, he quickly took charge of the team. Under his leadership, the team became a big gate attraction.

Posey built his powerful team in part by raiding other teams for quality ballplayers. Eventually Gus Greenlee turned the tables on him and signed most

Satchel Paige loosens up before a game. A consummate entertainer, Paige would often demonstrate his control by using a matchbox or chewing-gum wrapper as his plate during warm-ups.

of Posey's best players. The loss of these stars resulted in some lean seasons for the Grays during the
heart of the Great Depression. In need of more
operating money, Posey decided to bring in a partner, choosing Rufus "Sonnyman" Jackson. With
Jackson's bankroll, Posey was able to attract Josh
Gibson back to the team in 1937.

Gibson joined with another Grays slugger, Buck
Leonard, to form a powerful long-ball duo that
earned the nickname "Thunder Twins" and was
referred to by the media as "the black Babe Ruth
and Lou Gehrig." Anchoring the Grays' fearsome
"murderers' row," a group of dangerous hitters, the
two sluggers were largely responsible for the team's
perennial success.

The Grays played their home games at Forbes
Field, home of the National League's Pittsburgh
Pirates, and at Griffith Stadium, home of the American League's Washington Senators. To his dismay,
Senators owner Clark Griffith watched Gibson and
Leonard hit more home runs in his ballpark than his
entire lowly team. Exasperated, he once summoned
the two Grays sluggers to his office after a game and
discussed the possibility of signing them to play with
the Senators. Both players assured him they would
welcome the opportunity. But ultimately Griffith
proved unwilling to be the first owner to break
major league baseball's color line, and the two future
Hall of Famers remained in the Negro leagues.

With Gibson and Leonard hammering home
runs, the Grays began their string of nine straight
pennants in 1937, the first year the two sluggers
played together. A newspaper wrote, "The Grays
boast a new superstar in Buck Leonard." But
Leonard said, "When we got Josh is when we starting winning. He made the whole team better."

Gibson was the hitter that all others are mea-
sured against. He hit for both power and average.
He is reported to have slammed 962 home runs in

17 seasons of play, although many of these were against lesser competition. In league competition he maintained a lifetime batting average of .354.

Gibson was just as electrifying behind the plate as he was in the batter's box. The big man had a rifle arm and made a name for himself as a terrific catcher. In fact, two of the greatest pitchers in baseball history, Walter Johnson and Carl Hubbell, considered Gibson to be among the best catchers ever. "He hits the ball a mile," said Johnson. "And he catches so easy he might as well be in a rocking chair." Johnson put his value at $200,000 at a time when the top major leaguers earned less than half that amount. By the time he ended his career, Gibson was arguably the best player ever at his position.

An easygoing man, Gibson was well liked by fans and peers and was consistently voted to the all-star team. While he continued to enjoy success in baseball, however, his personal life began to deteriorate. Excessive use of alcohol and possibly illicit

Buck Leonard, one-half of the Homestead Grays' "Thunder Twins" slugging duo, demonstrates his powerful swing during a 1944 game against the New York Cuban Stars at Griffith Stadium, home of the American League's Washington Senators. After seeing Leonard and his teammate Josh Gibson pound home runs, Senators owner Clark Griffith toyed with the idea of signing the two black stars to help his lowly team. But ultimately he was unwilling to break the "gentlemen's agreement" among major league baseball owners not to hire African Americans.

Josh Gibson, called "the black Babe Ruth," is reported to have hit 962 home runs in his 17-year career, including a 580-foot blast that nearly left Yankee Stadium. In Negro leagues competition he is credited with a lifetime batting average of .354.

drugs took a physical and psychological toll, and in January of 1943 he was committed to a hospital after experiencing a nervous breakdown.

His play on the field also suffered, and teammates and opponents alike noticed the change. By 1946, the once-powerful Gibson could hardly crouch behind the plate. Despite his physical deterioration, that season he crushed a 550-foot home run at Sportsman's Park in St. Louis.

After Jackie Robinson was signed by the Dodgers, Gibson had dreams of playing in the major leagues. Sadly, he never got the opportunity. On January 20, 1947, he died of a stroke at 35 years of age, just a few months before Robinson's major league debut. Gibson's untimely death was baseball's loss, and American sports fans would never witness his incredible talent in the major leagues.

The funeral was quiet, attended only by a small group of close friends and family members. Fittingly, one of the pallbearers was Buck Leonard, the other half of the "Thunder Twins" power tandem.

Buck Leonard was born in 1907 in Rocky Mount, North Carolina. When his father died in the influenza epidemic of 1919, Leonard had to quit school and go to work to help support his family. Later he secured a job placing brake cylinders on boxcars at the Atlantic Coastline Railroad Shop. It was then that Leonard began to play semipro baseball. For seven years he held down a full-time job while also starring for the local ballclub. But when the Depression hit, he lost his job and left home to pursue a professional baseball career.

During the 1933 season, he played for the Portsmouth Black Revels, the Baltimore Stars, and the Brooklyn Royal Giants. Eventually, Smokey Joe Williams saw him playing and put him in touch with the Homestead Grays. Leonard joined the Grays in 1934 and stayed with them until the team broke up in 1950.

Leonard was a great fastball hitter. Pitchers said that trying to sneak a fastball past him was like trying to sneak a sunrise past a rooster. The left-handed slugger averaged 34 home runs over an eight-year period. He was also a good fielder and a smart ballplayer who rarely made mistakes. Young players respected him because he was a consistent professional and a team player who led by example. The Grays enjoyed great success during Leonard's years with the club.

However, there were other good ballclubs in the league. The Newark Eagles and Baltimore Elite Giants battled the Grays for the top spot almost every year. On two occasions the New York Cubans (1941) and the Philadelphia Stars (1944) challenged as well.

In 1937 the Newark Eagles provided their stiffest opposition for the Grays. The Eagles featured a much-touted infield consisting of Ray Dandridge, Willie Wells, Dick Seay, and Mule Suttles.

Dandridge, a masterful third baseman, was smooth as silk in the field. One reporter remarked that he was so relaxed that he looked as if he were waiting on a streetcar. Another declared that a train could go between his bowlegs, but a baseball never did. Monte Irvin said, "People would have paid their way in to the game just to see him field." A few years later, Dandridge jumped to Mexico and became a national hero. Subsequently, he was elected to the Hall of Fame in both Mexico and the United States.

The Elites claimed the 1939 title because they won a four-team postseason tournament. Three years later they chased the Grays to the wire before losing in the final week of the stretch run. The club featured Bill Wright, Henry Kimbro, Sammy T. Hughes, Bill Byrd, and a young catcher named Roy Campanella. Wright was a big, fast, switch-hitting outfielder. Kimbro, also a speedy outfielder, was a good hitter. At second base, Hughes was a smooth fielder. Byrd, the ace of the pitching staff, specialized in throwing the spitball. And Campanella went on to star with the Brooklyn Dodgers after the color line was eliminated.

Somehow the Grays always managed to play well enough to win, and the constant presence of Buck Leonard in the lineup made the difference. His talents were so great that the Grays continued to win even when Josh Gibson jumped the club to play two years in Mexico.

In 1942 Gibson returned from Mexico, and the Grays faced Satchel Paige's Kansas City Monarchs

in the first Negro League World Series between the Negro American League and the Negro National League. The Monarchs took the series in four straight games, despite a heroic effort by Leonard, who played with a taped broken hand.

The Grays rebounded to win back-to-back Negro World Series titles in 1943 and 1944 over the Birmingham Black Barons, before losing the 1945 series to the upstart Cleveland Buckeyes, led by catcher-manager Quincey Trouppe and star outfielder Sam "The Jet" Jethroe.

The next year would not see the Grays in the Negro World Series. The 1946 Newark Eagles, led by Monte Irvin, Larry Doby, and Leon Day—who were all returning from service in World War II—ended the Grays' string of nine straight pennants. Day pitched an opening day no-hitter and went on to top the league in victories and strikeouts. Monte Irvin said, "If we had one game to win, we wanted Leon to pitch." Irvin and Doby, who went on to later stardom in the major leagues, headed a power-

Giving new meaning to the term "must-win situation": In 1937 eight Negro leagues stars—front row: Leroy Matlock (second from left), Cool Papa Bell (middle), Sam Bankhead (third from right); middle row: Satchel Paige (right); back row: Josh Gibson (left), Chester Williams (second from left), Bob Griffith (third from right), and Bill Perkins (right)—traveled to the Dominican Republic to play on the Ciudad Trujillo team of dictator Rafael Trujillo, who hoped to stem discontent with his regime by producing a championship club. Before the deciding game, team manager Lazaro Salazar (middle row, left) warned his players that they might be executed if they lost. They won.

ful lineup that also included Lennie Pearson and Johnny Davis.

While the Grays were dominating the Negro National League in the east, Satchel Paige and the Kansas City Monarchs took control of the Negro American League in the west. Paige had joined Kansas City after one of the most bizarre interludes of his long and colorful career. After starring with the Pittsburgh Crawfords in 1936, he had gone to play in the Dominican Republic early the following year, lured by the promise of splitting $30,000 with seven other top black players, including Josh Gibson and Cool Papa Bell. The Negro leagues stars were to play a short 31-game season for the team of Rafael Trujillo, the Caribbean nation's embattled dictator. Facing widespread discontent with his regime, Trujillo hoped to regain the support of his baseball-loving people by producing a championship team.

When they arrived in the Dominican Republic's capital, Santo Domingo (which the dictator had recently renamed Ciudad Trujillo in his own honor), the Americans had no idea how high the stakes were. Trujillo had arranged for them to be housed in a private club, away from the Dominican people and their Ciudad Trujillo teammates. But soon the seriousness of the situation became apparent. During games, they played under the watchful eye of armed guards. Once, before a big game, the players were even locked in jail to prevent them from drinking, and it was said that Trujillo had vowed to execute any Dominican caught providing the Americans with whiskey.

Competition in the Dominican league was stiff, as Trujillo's opponents had also recruited Negro leagues stars for their teams in hopes of winning the championship and making the dictator look bad. But the Ciudad Trujillo team of Latin and black players gelled, winning a string of games and advancing to the championship against the Estrellas de Oriente.

Before the deciding game, Ciudad Trujillo manager Lazaro Salazar warned his club that they might all be executed if they failed to win. For a while, it did not look good. Going into the seventh inning, the Estrellas held a one-run lead, but Ciudad Trujillo rallied to score two runs and take the lead. Satchel Paige, who would later talk about the unique inspiration that the sight of machine-gun-toting soldiers provided, shut out the Estrellas the rest of the game. Paige and his teammates escaped with a 6-5 victory, and Trujillo had his championship.

Upon his return to the United States, Paige found himself banned from the Negro leagues. He responded by forming a team of his own and spent the remainder of the year barnstorming across the country. Invariably, his club attracted larger crowds than the league teams.

In 1938 Paige pitched in another country whose people loved *el beisbol*: Mexico. There he developed a sore arm, which led experts to predict that his pitching days were finally over. Undaunted, he signed on with the Kansas City Monarchs' traveling "B" team as a gate attraction. Amazingly, his arm healed during this period and his comeback was on.

In 1939 he joined the Monarchs as a regular player and pitched the team to the first of four consecutive Negro American League pennants (1939–1942), culminating in a clean sweep of the Homestead Grays in the 1942 Negro World Series. Paige won three of those games himself, including the clincher. He was, however, outpitched in one game by Leon Day, whom the Grays had picked up as a "ringer." Because Day was not on the Grays' roster and was therefore not eligible to pitch, the victory was disallowed, and Paige nailed down the series in his next outing.

Pitcher Leon Day of the Newark Eagles was picked up as a "ringer" by the Homestead Grays on the eve of their 1942 Negro World Series matchup with the Kansas City Monarchs. Though he beat Satchel Paige in one of the games, Day's victory was disallowed, and the Monarchs swept the series.

When the United States entered World War II, many of the Monarchs' key players were drafted, and the team fell on lean times. After the war, however, Kansas City returned to its winning ways, capturing a fifth pennant in 1946 before being out-lasted by the Newark Eagles in a seven-game Negro World Series.

Although Satchel Paige was the star of the ball-club, the Monarchs were hardly a one-man team. They had one of the deepest pitching staffs in Negro leagues history, with Paige himself frequently being relieved after the third inning by Hilton Smith, who thereby earned the nickname "Satchel's Shadow." The Monarchs also had gifted position players. Foremost among these were Willard Brown, Buck O'Neil, and Ted Strong. Brown was a talented slug-ger, O'Neil a sterling defensive first baseman who won the batting title in 1946. Strong, who also played basketball with the well-known Harlem Globetrotters, was a versatile player and a good hitter.

These Monarchs stars were frequently spotlight-ed in the East-West Game, which continued to be a highlight of each season. With the new league setup, the West squad was composed of players from the Negro American League, while the East squad came from the Negro National League.

The Monarchs' Hilton Smith was the losing pitcher in the 1937 game but returned the following year to pitch the West to a 5-4 victory. The 1939 game furnished a dramatic climax when Dan Wil-son of the St. Louis Stars hit a two-run homer in the bottom of the eighth inning to give pitcher Double Duty Radcliffe and the West a 4-2 win. In 1940 the East roared back with a vengeance, pounding a dozen hits to take an 11-0 victory. This was the most lopsided contest in the classic's history and evened the victories at four games apiece.

Between 1941 and 1943, attendance at the East-

West Game averaged more than 50,000, with the highest mark coming in 1943 at 51,723. Because of the popularity of the contest, it was not unusual for one game to be played at Comiskey Park and a second game to be played at another location in the East. As rumors circulated about the possibility of dropping the color line, many major league scouts began watching these games with an eye toward the future.

In 1941 Buck Leonard hammered a home run and knocked in three runs to power the East to an 8-3 win. The next year the East added a 5-2 victory, with Dave Barnhill getting the win and Satchel Paige taking the loss. But the star of that game was Leon Day, who saved the game by fanning five of the seven batters he faced, including the final four in succession. Earlier that season, Day had fanned 18 batters (including Roy Campanella three times) to set the league record for strikeouts.

In a rematch the following year, Paige took a 2-1 pitching duel over Barnhill. This was Paige's second all-star victory, making him the first pitcher to win more than one East-West Game. That mark was soon matched by Verdell Mathis, a slender Memphis Red Sox left-hander who started and won back-to-back victories for the West in the 1944 and 1945 games. The West also won the contest in 1946—and in the next two years, but by then the Negro leagues' days were numbered.

7

End of an Era (1947–1960)

History is made as Jackie Robinson signs a contract with a farm club of the Brooklyn Dodgers, thus becoming the first African American in organized professional baseball in more than 60 years. Brooklyn owner Branch Rickey, who was determined to integrate the major leagues, is at left. Robinson's success on the field and his dignified bearing in the face of venomous racism ensured that other black players would get the opportunity to play in the major leagues—and ultimately spelled the end of the Negro leagues.

IF 1947 WAS the year everything changed for major league baseball, it also marked a less dramatic, though undeniable, turning point for the Negro leagues. When Jackie Robinson took the field for the Brooklyn Dodgers, major league baseball's 63-year-old color line was crossed in what was referred to as a noble experiment. Robinson's stellar play and his dignified restraint in the face of enormous pressure and racist abuse ensured that the experiment would succeed. As a rapt nation watched, the second baseman who had grown up in Pasadena, California, proved to even the most skeptical critics that blacks did belong at baseball's highest levels, thus opening the door to the major leagues for other talented African-American ballplayers.

Though full integration would come slowly to the major leagues, the process was inexorable, making the demise of the Negro leagues only a matter of time. As more and more black stars left the Negro leagues for the majors, fans and the press gradually followed. The owners found themselves in growing financial straits, and many clubs were dissolved. Although a few teams played on, by 1950 the Negro leagues were no longer of major league quality.

None of this was evident at the start of the 1947

season, however. As the eyes of the nation focused on Jackie Robinson and the drama being played out in Brooklyn and the other baseball cities of the National League, the Negro leagues embarked on another summer of baseball.

The Newark Eagles, fresh off a Negro National League pennant and a Negro World Series championship, started the 1947 season well. But when the club faltered during the second half of the season, the New York Cubans made their move. The Cubans went on to capture the pennant behind the pitching of David Barnhill and Luis Tiant, Sr., whose son later starred in the major leagues.

The lineups of the following year's East-West Game graphically illustrate the inevitability of the Negro leagues' demise. Nine of the all-stars in the 1948 classic—Monte Irvin, Luke Easter, Minnie Minoso, Junior Gilliam, Luis Marquez, Willard Brown, Bob Boyd, Artie Wilson, and Quincey Trouppe—would later play in the major leagues.

As the 1948 season wore on, Buck Leonard emerged yet again to lead the Homestead Grays to one final Negro National League pennant. He finished the year with the league batting title and tied for the lead in home runs. In the Negro World Series, the Grays defeated the Birmingham Black Barons, who featured playing manager Piper Davis and a teenaged center fielder named Willie Mays.

After the 1948 season, the Negro National League disbanded, and Buck Leonard eventually found his way to Mexico. In 1952, in the twilight of his career, he was offered the chance to play in the major leagues by St. Louis Browns owner Bill Veeck. By then Leonard knew it was too late for him. He remained in the Mexican League until his retirement from baseball at the age of 48.

In 1972 Buck Leonard was inducted into the National Baseball Hall of Fame along with Josh Gibson. "It seems like we always did everything

Catcher Roy Campanella, who broke into the Negro leagues as a teenager, went from the Baltimore Elite Giants to the Brooklyn Dodgers and won three Most Valuable Player awards.

together," Leonard remarked. "We even went into the Hall of Fame at the same time."

The initial impetus to integrate the major leagues had come largely from Branch Rickey, the Brooklyn Dodgers' team president. After settling on Jackie Robinson as the ideal candidate to break the color line, Rickey set about searching the Negro leagues for other black stars to make the transition to the major leagues. At first, he wanted to find an African-American player to room with Robinson to deflect some of the pressure. He chose Johnny Wright, a right-handed pitcher with the Homestead Grays. Wright accompanied Robinson to the spring training camp of the Montreal Royals, Brooklyn's farm team, in 1946. Unfortunately, he seemed

Larry Doby of the Cleveland Indians, the first black player in the American League, heads for first base in a game against the Philadelphia Athletics on July 12, 1947. Doby had starred for the Negro leagues' Newark Eagles club.

unable to withstand the pressures that the two barrier breakers faced and failed to perform up to his potential. Wright was subsequently dropped to a lower classification and eventually returned to the Negro leagues.

He was replaced by Philadelphia Stars left-hander Roy Partlow, who was talented but temperamental. Although he pitched well for the Dodgers' farm clubs, he encountered difficulties and left the organization to return to the Stars.

Rickey, still looking for a black pitcher, personally scouted Dan Bankhead of the Memphis Red Sox, a hard-throwing right-hander who was viewed as another Satchel Paige. Impressed by what he saw, Rickey bought his contract for $15,000, a rather high amount for that time. Bankhead went straight to the major leagues with the Dodgers, where he had the honor of being the first black pitcher to play in the major leagues. He had the further distinction of hitting a home run in his first at-bat in the majors.

But that bright beginning was short lived. Bankhead experienced control problems and was sent to the minor leagues for seasoning. He returned to the Dodgers in 1950 and earned a spot in the regular rotation. But a sore shoulder ended his major league career after only three seasons, although he continued to pitch in Canada and Mexico for several more years.

Rickey remained committed to bringing black ballplayers into the major leagues and continued to sign young black prospects. He acquired Roy Campanella from the Baltimore Elite Giants and Don Newcombe from the Newark Eagles with the idea that they would room together. In 1946 they played at Nashua and eventually worked their way to the parent Dodger team. Campanella arrived in 1948; Newcombe, a year later, when he won Rookie of the Year honors.

Both players became stars and were instrumental in the Dodgers' pennants during the years when the Brooklyn team became the celebrated "Boys of Summer." Along the way, Campanella won three Most Valuable Player awards (1951, 1953, 1955), and Newcombe added one (1956).

Campanella, who was inducted into the Hall of Fame for his outstanding career, had started in the Negro leagues as a teenager in 1937. By the time Rickey signed him, he was an established veteran; he could easily have gone into the majors as early as 1941 had the door been open to him. Newcombe was still a youngster when he signed with the Dodgers and had almost his entire baseball career in front of him.

Rickey also had signed Monte Irvin from the Newark Eagles, but when owner Effa Manley demanded compensation for her player and threatened legal action, the Dodgers executive relinquished his claim. This permitted the New York Giants to sign Irvin in a move that he called "the best thing that ever happened to me."

The Giants sent Irvin, Hank Thompson, and pitcher Ford Smith to their Jersey City farm club. After a season there, Irvin and Thompson moved up to the major league ballclub in 1949 to become the first black players on the Giants. Irvin had a sensational season and helped lead the Giants to the 1951 pennant.

Earlier in his career, he had been voted by the Negro National League owners to be the player most likely to break the color line. But Irvin left baseball to serve his country in World War II, and by the time he returned from the army, Rickey had already selected Jackie Robinson for that role.

After the success of Irvin and Thompson, the New York Giants pursued two more players from the Negro leagues. In 1949 owner Horace Stoneham signed veteran third baseman Ray Dandridge and pitcher David Barnhill from the New York Cubans. The pair were assigned to the Minneapolis Millers, the Giants' AAA farm club, and in 1950 they led the Millers to the league championship, with Dandridge taking the league's MVP honors. A year later they were joined by Willie Mays. Though the Giants never brought either of the veterans to the major leagues, they did call up Mays.

At that time many major league teams were maintaining an unofficial quota system for black ballplayers, and when Mays was signed, Artie Wilson, a former Birmingham Black Barons shortstop who had joined the Giants for a short stint, was sent back to the minors to make room for Mays.

Piper Davis, Mays' mentor and Wilson's teammate on the Black Barons, had been signed by the Boston Red Sox organization a few years earlier. But he never advanced beyond the AAA level, and

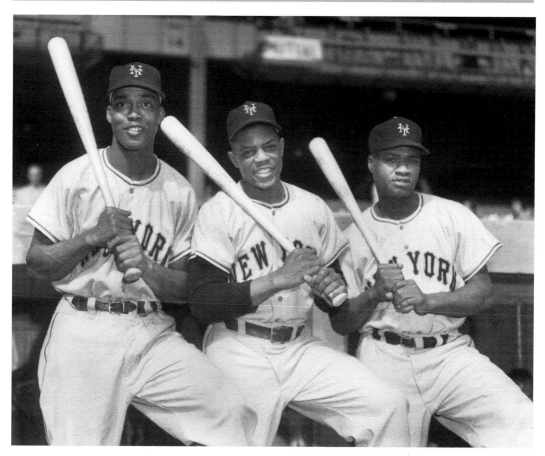

A trio of Negro leagues alumni formed a dream outfield for the New York Giants. From left: Monte Irvin, Willie Mays, Hank Thompson.

the Red Sox became the last team to integrate their major league club. Davis had been Willie Mays' manager on the Black Barons and had been instrumental in discovering and developing the young supertalent. During his subsequent career in organized ball, the versatile Davis showcased his talent by playing a different position each inning in both the Pacific Coast League and the Texas League.

Many observers felt that the Red Sox, whose major league team remained all white until 1959, were not sincere in trying to place a black player on the roster. In 1945 the team had arranged a "tryout" for Jackie Robinson, Marvin Williams, and Sam Jethroe. Although the players performed well, they were not pursued by the Sox.

Subsequently, Jethroe was signed by the Dodgers and then traded to the Boston Braves. Like many Negro leaguers, The Jet shaved several years off his official age to improve his chances of making the major leagues. In 1950 the former Cleveland Buckeye outfielder was the National League Rookie of the Year. For the next three years the award was won by former Negro leagues players—Willie Mays, Joe Black, and Junior Gilliam—to give former Negro leaguers that distinction for five straight years and six of the first seven years the award was given.

While Branch Rickey took the initiative in integrating the National League, Cleveland Indians owner Bill Veeck acted as his counterpart in the American League. In 1947, the same year that Jackie Robinson made his major league debut, Veeck signed Larry Doby as the first black player in the American League. Doby went directly from the Negro leagues' Newark Eagles to the Indians and enjoyed a long and successful major league career.

Soon after Doby's debut, St. Louis Browns general manager Bill DeWitt signed two players from the Kansas City Monarchs, Willard Brown and Hank Thompson, in an attempt to bring more fans to Sportsman's Park. Like Doby, the pair went directly to the major leagues. But unlike Doby, they failed to perform up to expectations and also failed to bring in the extra fans that DeWitt had anticipated. Both players were released and returned to the Monarchs. Two years later Hank Thompson proved his ability when he was signed by the New York Giants and went on to have a good nine-year major league career.

Meanwhile, in 1948 Bill Veeck signed the ageless Satchel Paige to join Doby on the Cleveland Indians roster. As the oldest rookie ever to play major league baseball (he is believed to have been born in 1906), he registered a 6-1 record and a 2.48

Satchel Paige, photographed in 1972 on the day he became the first Negro leagues star inducted into the National Baseball Hall of Fame.

earned run average down the stretch to help pitch the Indians to the pennant and a World Series victory that year.

Within two years, both Veeck and Paige had left the Indians, but in 1951 they were reunited on the St. Louis Browns when Veeck bought the franchise and signed Paige. Veeck, the consummate showman, used Satchel's age as a drawing card, providing him with a rocking chair in the bullpen, where the hurler relaxed when not in action. During his stint with the Browns, Paige made appearances in the major league All-Star Games of 1952 and 1953.

Players who had started in the Negro leagues continued to enter major league baseball and become stars. In 1954 both Ernie Banks and Hank Aaron made their major league debuts. Banks had played with the Kansas City Monarchs, Aaron with the Indianapolis Clowns.

The Clowns, who were the Harlem Globetrotters of baseball, were the last quality black team. Because of their unique combination of baseball and "show biz," they continued to draw good crowds. Although the overall quality of the league had declined, the Clowns won four Negro American League pennants in the first half of the 1950s.

During this time, owner Syd Pollock signed three female players, marking the first time that women had played with men at that level of competition. In 1953 second baseman Toni Stone became the first of the female ballplayers. She would usually play three innings and then be removed from the game. Many observers thought that she was being used primarily as a gate attraction, and indeed, her presence piqued the interest of the paying public.

A year later second baseman Connie Morgan and pitcher Mamie Johnson signed with the Clowns, while Stone moved to the Kansas City Monarchs. The Clowns continued barnstorming across the country into the 1970s, long after the Negro American League had finally dissolved, almost unnoticed by fans and the media, in 1960.

With the influx of a vast new pool of talent, it was inevitable that the major leagues would expand to add new teams. Many authorities insist that the best baseball ever played was during the years between integration and expansion, when the existing teams were adding talented black players to their rosters.

As the years passed, more and more African-American players made it to the major leagues without having first played in the Negro leagues. And gradually, the ballplayers who had begun their careers in the Negro leagues retired from the game. Memories began to fade of the long-ago summers when, barred from taking the field with their white peers, black men with names like Foster, Day, and Wells, Leonard, Bell, and Gibson played the game away from the glare of the spotlight but with unsurpassed skill and enthusiasm. Those men and their vibrant, vital leagues have captured the imagination of baseball fans everywhere and have become the stuff of legends.

In 1965, at the dubious age of 59, Satchel Paige added another chapter to his legend as he pitched three innings for the Kansas City Athletics, thus becoming the oldest man ever to pitch in a major league game. When Paige finally hung up his spikes for the last time, he estimated that he had pitched 2,600 games, 300 shutouts, and 55 no-hitters. As a fitting climax to his incredible baseball career, he was elected to the National Baseball Hall of Fame in 1971, becoming the first Negro leagues player to receive baseball's highest honor.

One of Satchel Paige's rules for longevity was "Don't look back; something might be gaining on you." Something finally caught up with him on June 8, 1982, when the great star passed away. With him passed a large measure of the magical spirit of the Negro leagues.

CHRONOLOGY

April 24, 1878	Bud Fowler becomes the first black professional baseball player when he pitches the Chelsea, Massachusetts, team to a 2-1 victory over the Boston Nationals
March 18, 1884	Moses Fleetwood Walker becomes the first black in the major leagues, playing catcher for the Toledo ballclub in the American Association
1885	The first black professional team, the Cuban Giants, is organized and begins touring
July 14, 1887	The International League's board of directors declares that no new black players will be allowed in the league, establishing an official "color line" for the first time in professional baseball
July 19, 1887	Cap Anson refuses to allow his National League champion Chicago White Sox to play an exhibition game against Newark's ace black pitcher George Stovey
Spring 1889	Two black teams, the New York Gorhams and the Cuban Giants, join the Middle States League, marking the first time in the history of organized baseball that a black team has appeared in an otherwise all-white league
Fall 1903	The Cuban X-Giants defeat the Philadelphia Giants for the Negro Championship as Rube Foster pitches four victories in the seven-game series
September 3, 1906	The Philadelphia Giants win the Negro Championship Cup before 10,000 fans, the largest crowd that had ever attended a black baseball game
October 27, 1912	New York Lincoln Giants ace Cyclone Joe Williams shuts out the National League champion New York Giants, 6-0, while fanning nine batters
October 15, 1915	Lincoln Giants hurler Joe Williams fans 10 batters on the way to a five-hit, 1-0 shutout of the National League champion Philadelphia Phillies
February 13, 1920	The Negro National League (officially chartered as the

National Association of Colored Professional Baseball Clubs) is organized

May 2, 1920	The Indianapolis ABCs defeat the Chicago American Giants, 4-2, in the first Negro National League game
July 6, 1921	The Detroit Stars' Bill Gatewood pitches the first no-hitter in Negro National League history, defeating the Cuban Stars, 4-0
August 22, 1922	The Chicago American Giants defeat the Bacharach Giants of Atlantic City, 1-0, in a 20-inning game in which Dave Brown pitches the last 16 innings in relief to get the win, while Harold Treadwell, who goes the entire distance, suffers the loss
December 16, 1922	The Eastern Colored League (officially chartered as the Mutual Association of Eastern Colored Baseball Clubs) is organized
January 1923	The New York Lincoln Giants sign the Chicago American Giants' star pitcher, Dave Brown, thus starting a player war between the two Negro leagues
October 1924	The Kansas City Monarchs of the Negro National League defeat the Eastern Colored League's Hilldale club in the first Negro World Series
September 29, 1926	Willie Foster tosses double shutouts over the Kansas City Monarchs, 1-0 and 5-0, in the final-day twin bill of the Negro National League Championship Series to give the Chicago American Giants the pennant
October 3, 1926	The Bacharach Giants' Red Grier pitches a 10-0 no-hitter against the Chicago American Giants in the third game of the Negro World Series
1928	The Eastern Colored League folds
1929	The American Negro League replaces the Eastern Colored League but folds after one season
July 5, 1930	In the first games ever played between two black teams at

	Yankee Stadium, 20,000 fans see the New York Lincoln Giants and the Baltimore Black Sox split a doubleheader
August 1, 1930	Josh Gibson appears in his first game for the Homestead Grays
December 9, 1930	Rube Foster, "the Father of the Negro Leagues," dies
1931	The Negro National League folds
1932	Cum Posey spearheads the formation of the East-West League, which folds in midseason
January 1933	The new Negro National League is organized under the leadership of Pittsburgh Crawfords owner Gus Greenlee
September 10, 1933	The first Negro leagues East-West All-Star Game is played, with the West winning, 11-7, behind the pitching of Willie Foster
July 4, 1934	Satchel Paige pitches a 4-0 no-hitter against the Homestead Grays in Pittsburgh, travels to Chicago, and shuts out the Chicago American Giants, 1-0, in 12 innings—giving him two shutouts in two different cities on the same day
September 9, 1934	In the second game of a four-team doubleheader at Yankee Stadium, Satchel Paige of the Pittsburgh Crawfords and Slim Jones of the Philadelphia Stars battle to a 1-1 stalemate that is halted after nine innings because of darkness; some authorities consider it the most memorable game in the history of black baseball
August 11, 1935	Mule Suttles' home run off Martin Dihigo in the bottom of the 11th inning gives the West an 11-8 victory in the East-West Game
1937	The Negro American League, with teams in the Midwest and South, plays its inaugural season
August 18, 1940	After being walked in his first two plate appearances, Buck Leonard hammers three straight hits to pace the

East squad to a lopsided 11-0 victory over the West in the East-West Game

1942   Baseball commissioner Judge Landis issues a statement that there is no rule or agreement to keep blacks out of the major leagues; the Kansas City Monarchs sweep the Homestead Grays in the first World Series between the Negro National League and the Negro American League

1944   The Homestead Grays become the only team to win consecutive Negro World Series championships

October 23, 1945   Brooklyn Dodgers owner Branch Rickey announces the signing of Jackie Robinson

May 5, 1946   Newark Eagles ace Leon Day, returning after two years of military service, pitches an opening-day no-hitter to defeat the Philadelphia Stars, 2-0

April 15, 1947   Jackie Robinson breaks major league baseball's "color barrier," playing second base for the Brooklyn Dodgers in a 5-3 opening-day victory over the Boston Braves

July 5, 1947   Larry Doby becomes the first black to play in the American League, pinch-hitting for the Cleveland Indians

1948   The Homestead Grays win the final Negro World Series; the Negro National League folds

1960   The Negro American League folds

FURTHER READING

Ashe, Arthur R., Jr. *A Hard Road to Glory—Baseball: The African American Athlete in Baseball.* New York: Amistad Books, 1993.

Bruce, Janet. *The Kansas City Monarchs: Champions of Black Baseball.* Lawrence: University Press of Kansas, 1985.

Clark, Dick, and Lester, Larry. *The Negro Leagues Book.* Cleveland, OH: The Society for American Baseball Research, 1994.

Dixon, Phil S., and Hannigan, Patrick. *The Negro Baseball Leagues: A Photographic History, 1867–1955.* Mattituck, NY: Amereon House, 1992.

Holway, John B. *Blackball Stars: Negro League Pioneers.* New York: Carroll & Graf, 1992.

_____. *Black Diamonds.* Westport, CT: Meckler, 1989.

Irvin, Monte, and Riley, James A. *Nice Guys Finish First.* New York: Carroll & Graf, 1996.

Malloy, Jerry. *Sol White's History of Colored Base Ball with Other Documents on the Early Black Game, 1886–1936.* Lincoln: The University of Nebraska Press, 1995.

Paige, LeRoy, and Lipman, David. *Maybe I'll Pitch Forever.* Lincoln: University of Nebraska Press, 1993.

Paige, LeRoy, and Lebovitz, Hal. *Pitchin' Man.* Westport, CT: Meckler, 1992.

Peterson, Robert. *Only the Ball Was White: A History of Legendary Black Players and All-Black Professional Teams.* Englewood Cliffs, NJ: Prentice-Hall Publishers, 1970.

Ribowsky, Mark. *Don't Look Back: Satchel Paige in the Shadows of Baseball.* New York: Simon & Schuster, 1994.

Riley, James A. *The All-Time All-Stars of Black Baseball.* Cocoa, FL: TK Publishers, 1983.

_____. *The Biographical Encyclopedia of the Negro Baseball Leagues.* New York: Carroll & Graf, 1994.

_____. *Dandy, Day and the Devil.* Cocoa, FL: TK Publishers, 1987.

Riley, James A., and Leonard, Buck. *Buck Leonard: The Black Lou Gehrig.* New York: Carroll & Graf, 1995.

Rogosin, Donn. *Invisible Men: Life in Baseball's Negro Leagues.* New York: Atheneum, 1983.

INDEX

INDEX

PICTURE CREDITS

JAMES A. RILEY, a leading authority on the history of baseball's Negro leagues, is Director of Research for the Negro Leagues Baseball Museum in Kansas City, Missouri. His landmark reference volume, *The Biographical Encyclopedia of the Negro Baseball Leagues* (1994), is recognized as the most comprehensive work chronicling this era of baseball history. He has also written *The All-Time All-Stars of Black Baseball* (1983) and *Dandy, Day and the Devil* (1987) and coauthored (with Buck Leonard) *Buck Leonard: The Black Lou Gehrig* (1995). His collaboration with Hall of Famer Monte Irvin (*Monte Irvin: Nice Guys Finish First)* was released in the spring of 1996.

Mr. Riley has contributed to many compilations, including *Insiders Baseball* (1983), *Biographical Dictionary of American Sports: Baseball* (1987) and the 1989–92 and 1992–95 supplements of the *Biographical Dictionary of American Sports, The Ballplayers* (1990), *Baseball Chronology* (1991), and *African-American Sports Greats: A Biographical Dictionary* (1995). He has also contributed to *The Baseball Research Journal* (1981, 1982, 1985, 1991), *Oldtyme Baseball News* (1989–95), *Negro Leagues Baseball Museum Yearbook* (1993–94), *The Diamond* (1993–94), *Athlon Baseball* (1994, 1995), and *All-Star Game: Official Major League Baseball Program* (1993, 1994). In addition, he has served as an editor of the Negro leagues section of *The Baseball Encyclopedia* (1990). In 1990 and 1994 he was a recipient of the SABR-Macmillan Research Award for his scholarship on the Negro leagues.

Mr. Riley counts among his forebears frontiersman Daniel Boone, President Andrew Johnson, and an obscure Cherokee named Crow. The transplanted Tennessean and his wife, Dottie, reside in Rockledge, Florida.